MEDICINAL HERBS OF THE ROCKY MOUNTAINS

A Field Guide to Common Healing Plants

Blake Burger

Autumn in Spearfish Canyon, South Dakota
Jen Toews

DENVER BOTANIC
GARDENS
FALCON GUIDES

ESSEX, CONNECTICUT

FALCONGUIDES®

An imprint of Globe Pequot, the trade division of The Rowman & Littlefield Publishing Group, Inc.
4501 Forbes Blvd., Ste. 200
Lanham, MD 20706
www.rowman.com

Falcon and FalconGuides are registered trademarks and Make Adventure Your Story is a trademark of The Rowman & Littlefield Publishing Group, Inc.

Distributed by NATIONAL BOOK NETWORK

British Library Cataloguing in Publication Information available

Library of Congress Cataloging-in-Publication Data available

Names: Burger, Blake, author.
Title: Medicinal herbs of the Rocky Mountains : a field guide to common
  healing plants / Blake Burger.
Description: Guilford, Connecticut : Falcon, [2022] | Includes
  bibliographical references. | Summary: "Introduces the principles of
  herbal remedies and guides readers through finding, harvesting,
  cultivating, and incorporating more than 66 locally abundant medicinal
  plants into daily life"— Provided by publisher.
Identifiers: LCCN 2021060463 (print) | LCCN 2021060464 (ebook) | ISBN
  9781493060122 (paperback) | ISBN 9781493060139 (epub)
Subjects: LCSH: Medicinal plants—Rocky Mountains. | Herbs—Therapeutic
  use—Rocky Mountains. | Field guides.
Classification: LCC RS172.R63 B87 2022 (print) | LCC RS172.R63 (ebook) |
  DDC 615.3/210978—dc23/eng/20220121
LC record available at https://lccn.loc.gov/2021060463
LC ebook record available at https://lccn.loc.gov/2021060464

♾™ The paper used in this publication meets the minimum requirements of American National Standard for Information Sciences—Permanence of Paper for Printed Library Materials, ANSI/NISO Z39.48-1992.

CONTENTS

ACKNOWLEDGMENTS

The opportunity to write this book stems from a combination of passion, hard work, privilege, and sheer luck. I would like to thank and acknowledge the people in my life who helped me become an author of an actual, real, readable, published book. I would like to thank my grandmother for putting me to work in her beautiful garden at a young age. She instructed me to perfectly space red impatiens along the border of her beautiful woodland garden in Illinois. Once finished, I remember admiring the little red flowers against the backdrop of verdant shrubs and towering trees. I consider those plantings my first successful gardening moment. I would like to thank my mom for giving me my first medicinal plant encyclopedia for Christmas in 2009. That book lit a fire within me, sparking my interest in healing plants and self-care. Without the help of Jen Toews and Cindy Newlander, who edited my initial draft, this book would lack coherence, proper punctuation, and organization. Thank you for your support and hard work needed to complete this book. Thank you to each and every person who contributed their photographs for this book. Thank you, Anna Kongs, for your research and contributions to this book. And thank you to Denver Botanic Gardens, a beautiful oasis within the city of Denver and my place of work since 2007. Finally, I would like to thank Cat Pantaleo, Kim Thompson, and Martin Hansen for your passionate life-changing teachings about healing plants.

Wyethia arizonica
Mike Kintgen © Denver Botanic Gardens

We begin this guidebook by gratefully acknowledging the Indigenous peoples of the Rocky Mountain region. The Apache, Arapaho, Shoshone, Ute, Cherokee, Crow, Cheyenne, Chippewa, Pueblo, Apache, and countless other tribes call this land their home. You are the original stewards of the Rocky Mountains, cultivating a deep, harmonious relationship with the land, animals, and plants of this region for thousands and thousands of years. This guidebook includes information on the uses of medicinal plants by the many Indigenous peoples of the Rocky Mountains. We would like to thank you for your contribution to, and influence on, modern herbalism and modern medicine. We have all benefited from your alliance and understanding of plants, and the willingness to share your stories, healing methods, and medicine

Echinocereus growing in piñon-juniper woodland
Michael Guidi

with the rest of the world. These nations and communities are not a relic of the past; they exist today. It is our sincere hope that the legacy of your ancient culture continues to speak louder than the legacy of oppressive colonialism.

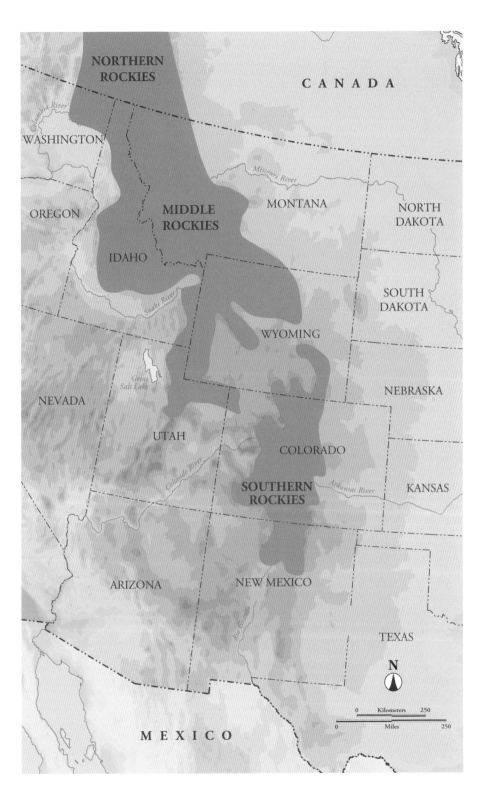

INTRODUCTION TO
THE ROCKY MOUNTAIN REGION

The immense and breathtaking Rocky Mountains showcases some of the best scenery North America has to offer. The majestic mountain range spans nearly 3,000 miles long (4,800 km) from northern British Columbia to New Mexico. In some areas, the Rocky Mountain range spreads 300 miles wide. The highest peak, Mount Elbert, measures at 14,433 feet and towers well above the grasslands and foothills below. The land is abundant with natural resources including coal, petroleum, precious metals, and natural gas. The Rockies' wildlife features some of North America's largest land mammals, including grizzly bear, moose, and bison, as well as an impressive array of birds of prey, smaller mammals, and fish. The plant life in the Rockies is equally impressive, home to many species of trees, both evergreen and deciduous, dazzling wildflowers, orchids, grasses, and lichens. The numerous scenic regions of the Rocky Mountains draw millions of people to the area to live and visit each year.

An American black bear foraging at Rocky Mountain National Park
Jen Toews

LIFE ZONES

A life zone is defined as a region characterized by specific plants and animals that inhabit the area. The Rocky Mountain region is home to six life zones. Each of these life zones has its own unique variety of flora and fauna. In this guidebook, the life zones are defined by elevation, but in nature, there are always exceptions to the rule, and these life zones can be blurred, especially at their edges. Also, within each of these regions there are unique land features such as canyons, rivers, ponds, and forests which create microclimates and habitats that may deviate from the life zone's assumed characteristics.

Grasslands/Plains

The area located east of the Rocky Mountains is characterized by flat, expansive land with elevations ranging from 3,000 to 6,000 feet. The flora consists of many species of short grasses, drought-tolerant wildflowers such as *Penstemon* and *Rudbeckia*, and succulents such as *Yucca* and cacti. Trees and shrubs grow sporadically and are most prevalent and diverse near water sources. In undisturbed and semidisturbed sites, wildflowers thrive, especially in spring after the snow has melted and the ground is relatively moist. The plains receives a range of 12 to 18 inches of precipitation per year, although an occasional winter storm or thunderstorm may bring heavy rain and snow. The plains experience a wide range in temperatures, from 0 to 100 degrees F. Rivers and streams are scarce.

The eastern plains of Colorado
Jen Toews

Semidesert Shrublands

The semidesert life zone of the Southern Rockies encompasses the Western Slope and mountain parks of Colorado. Like its name suggests, semidesert shrublands are covered by a variety of shrubs, graminoids, and forbs. Its elevation can range from around 5,000 feet to 7,000 feet. The amount of precipitation that falls here is similar to the plains, ranging from 12 to 18 inches a year. Sprawling hillsides of sagebrush dominate areas with lower precipitation, providing rich habitat for many species of birds, butterflies, and other insects. Saltbush (*Atriplex* spp.) and greasewood (*Sarcobatus vermiculatus*) blanket much of the semidesert landscape as well. Temperatures in the region can range from well below freezing in the winter to nearly 100 degrees F.

Semidesert shrubland east of Moab, Utah
Michael Guidi

Foothills

The foothills life zone is characterized by rolling hills, cliffs and canyons, and riparian areas. Elevations vary from 6,000 to 8,000 feet. Mountain mahogany, chokecherry, and other shrubs are prevalent. At lower elevations scrub oak, piñon pines, and juniper thrive. At higher elevations ponderosa pine, blue spruce, and Douglas-fir are present. Wildflowers typically bloom in May or June. Snow provides ample amounts of moisture in the winter but typically melts by early to mid-spring. Precipitation amounts vary greatly depending on elevation and

Late spring in the foothills of the Rocky Mountains
Jen Toews

locations. Temperatures range from 80 to 90 degrees in the summer and below freezing in the winter.

Montane

The montane life zone ranges from 8,000 to 10,000 feet and contains a diversity of trees, shrubs, flowers, grasses, and graminoids. South-facing forests are typically aspen stands and ponderosa pine, while moisture-rich forests of Douglas-fir, lodgepole pine, and spruce are common on north-facing slopes. Deciduous trees such as alder, willow, and birch, and deciduous shrubs such as elder and currant also thrive in this life zone. Wildflowers typically bloom in June and peak in July. Microclimates and diverse habitats showcase an array of lush plant life.

Subalpine

The elevation of the subalpine life zone ranges from 10,000 feet to timberline in the Southern Rockies. In the Northern Rockies, treeline can be as low as 6,500 feet. At lower elevations of subalpine zones, lush forests of aspen, spruce, and pine are common. Subalpine fir and Engelmann spruce are the dominant community at higher elevations in many areas of the Rockies. Extreme weather and elevation may stunt the growth of many evergreens in this zone. Wildflowers bloom from late June into fall. During peak bloom, meadows and hillsides may

Montane intermountain park meadow with the Gore Range in the background; Middle Park, Colorado
Michael Guidi

Subalpine stream on Jones Pass, Arapaho National Forest, Colorado
Michael Guidi

Columbine comes from the Latin word *columba,* meaning dove-like; Butler Gulch, Arapaho National Forest, Colorado.
Michael Guidi

be painted with thousands of flowers. Cold winters are long and snow-packed, and frost or snow can occur at any time of the year. Temperatures rarely rise above 80 degrees F.

Alpine

Also known as tundra, this life zone begins at treeline, the point in a habitat where trees no longer grow. In the Southern Rockies, treeline begins around 11,500 feet, while in the Northern Rockies, treeline occurs around 6,500 feet. At higher latitudes, the elevation where the alpine life zone begins is lower. The alpine is characterized by high mountain summits, slopes, and rocky ridges that tower above treeline. The climate of this zone is characterized by thin, cold air, high winds, and intense solar radiation. Snowpack may cover some alpine areas until June or July, resulting in a very short growing season. Grasses and sedges dominate the landscape, and lichens and mosses are common. Dwarfed shrubs including willow, herbaceous perennials such as gentian, cushion plants, and other mat-forming plants grow in this life zone. Wildflowers bloom July through September.

IMPORTANCE OF HERBALISM

Today, we live in a world of miraculous medical and scientific advancement. At the end of 2019, humanity came face-to-face with an unfamiliar and deadly coronavirus, resulting in millions of deaths around the globe. Yet in just one year, the scientific community developed vaccines to slow the spread, severity, and death caused by COVID-19. Decade after decade, the pharmaceutical industry celebrates breakthroughs and advancements as it continues to invent medications capable of alleviating or curing some of humanity's deadliest and most detrimental diseases. With continued innovation and technology in the medical and health fields, where does herbalism fit in?

The answer to that question is: everywhere. While the world's health care system and medical technologies have evolved greatly over the past 100 years, we still need herbs close by. The herbs featured in the book, as well as hundreds of others, perform a wide range of duties for the human body and should not be discounted. Some herbs, like clover and nettle, provide ample amounts of vitamins and minerals to keep our body strong and healthy. Some herbs strengthen our systems, such as burdock which improves digestion and liver function, or elderberry, which builds immunity. Others, like valerian, sedate, while echinacea and rudbeckia can stimulate. Rather than create a dichotomy between "alternative medicine" and "modern medicine" which promotes conflict, we need to start merging the two. Herbal medicine's holistic approach can be combined with modern-day medicine. Rather than thinking of herbs as a substitution for a prescription drug or therapy, herbs can complement a treatment. One example is hawthorn. The berry or fruit of hawthorn is as safe as eating an apple, and the flavonoids present in the fruit that give it the red pigment are extremely beneficial for the heart. Medical studies have concluded that the antioxidants present in hawthorn can significantly improve heart function in patients with heart disease. While a physician may prescribe medications such as beta-blockers or antiplatelet therapy for specific heart conditions, an herbalist would likely recommend a hawthorn tincture. The conclusive medical studies of hawthorn as a safe herb with no drug interactions support its use as an adjunct therapy when fighting cardiovascular disease.

Imagine a world where our medical fields continue to make these technological advancements to improve health and eradicate disease, yet also embrace plants as equally effective in disease prevention and sustaining health; where doctors recommend gardening and forest bathing to relieve stress; prescribe oatstraw and nettle pre-surgery to build strength and to promote a quicker recovery; offer ragweed tincture to help with allergy season; and recommend motherwort for depression or sadness. Until this becomes commonplace, herbalists around the world will continue to keep this age-old tradition alive.

The medicinal plants featured in this text thrive and grow throughout the beautiful Rocky Mountain region. They dot the forest floors under towering aspens and spruce, grow happily between rock crevices, jagged cliffs, and gentle hillsides, and some prefer to spread their roots near rivers and streams fed by slowly melting snow. However, it is important to remember that a plethora of medicinal plants also thrive in our gardens, public parks and open spaces, and between the cracks in our sidewalks and in the alleys of cities. These beneficial and supportive plants are often growing right before our eyes, seemingly eager for interaction.

The practice and study of herbalism is a life-long endeavor, an endeavor that is accessible to all, no matter the neighborhood, economic status, age, gender, or education level. A harvesting trip to the foothills, a weed-gathering walk in your own backyard, or even a trip to your local grocery store is a worthwhile effort to supply you with enough plant material to make medicine. With a few inexpensive pantry staples and kitchen utensils on hand, you can transform a root, leaf, or seed into a remedy.

Artemisia tridentata, one of the most important ethnobotanical plants of the Rocky Mountain region; Middle Park, Colorado
Michael Guidi

By practicing herbalism, we are carrying on a tradition that dates back thousands of years. Humans have evolved with plants, and plants have evolved with humans. Prior to modern medicine, civilizations, tribes, and nations across the globe relied upon plants growing in their region to treat or cure a wide range of ailments. This practice dates back at least 60,000 years to the Paleolithic era. Since then, every civilization has practiced herbalism. It wasn't a hobby or a choice; it was a part of living and essential for survival. From the Ancient Greeks and Romans, to the Cherokee and Eskimo, the Shang Dynasty in China, and the native Aboriginal tribes of Australia, each had their own methods of processing plants into remedies.

Equally fascinating is the way these civilizations discovered which plants were medicinal and how to use them appropriately. The deserts and forests they lived near, habitat for thousands of species of plants, became their pharmacopeia. Ancient Egyptians, Greeks, and Indians left behind medical texts and documents which detailed uses for plants, complete with recipes and remedies for treatments of disease. One such document, the *Ebers Papyrus* out of Egypt, circa 1550 BC, contained recipes for insect repellents, birth control, and instructions on how to make a *Cannabis sativa* salve for inflammation.

As we study and compare these different medical texts of the past, we learn that civilizations spanning the globe and time used medicinal plants in similar ways. For example, yarrow was consistently utilized for its wound-healing properties by the Cheyenne in North America, Ancient Romans, and nomadic people of the Scottish Highlands. Plantain was used as a poison antidote in both Western Europe and in the American Southwest. This is hundreds if not thousands of years before globalization, the internet, or any effortless way these vastly different cultures could communicate with one another. Perhaps this is the result of generations of trial and error or the exchange of information as humans explored and settled across the world. Or was human intuition and their relationship to plants stronger and more connected than it is today?

Today, the collective consciousness of humans is waking up to the idea of a deeper connection with the Earth. Humans are realizing the importance of an existence that is more in tune and in balance with nature. The practice of herbalism can bring us one step closer. One way to achieve this is by learning the names of the plants in your region and observing their habitat. Pick a dandelion leaf on your next hike, close your eyes, and taste the earth and bitterness. Harvest a handful of fresh rosehips and brew a tea. Steep the flowers of arnica in oil. These simple activities bring us closer to our natural world. The more we learn about the plants growing in our environment, the tighter our bond to Mother Nature.

Keep this guidebook tucked away in your backpack and enjoy it on your next walk in the woods. During your hike, take a break and flip through the

Herbalism reinforces a deeper connection with the Earth.
Jen Toews

pages and start to familiarize yourself with the plants growing around you. This text can also be used as a recipe book, as many of the plant profiles include recipes and suggestions for incorporating these herbs into your diet and everyday life.

HARVESTING IN THE WILD

The flora of the Rocky Mountain region is incredibly diverse, with different plant communities inhabiting plains to alpine life zones. For centuries prior to industrialization and the arrival of European settlers, Arapaho, Ute, Crow, Navajo, and many other Native peoples lived in symbiosis with the plants, harvesting them for food, shelter, and medicine while ensuring their survival by thoughtful and sustainable practices. It was common tradition to ask a plant for permission before harvesting, sing to an herb, or spread seed to help the plant thrive. Today, through the lens of the human eye, this biodynamic region appears teeming with color, lush with plant life, and abundant with resources. And from a modern herbalist's perspective, the Rocky Mountains are rich in medicinal plants that continue to treat ailments, disease, and help strengthen the mind, body, and spirit.

However, it's important to remember these plants are delicate beings growing in an environment that is in a constant state of change. This change is both subtle and obvious—influenced by natural phenomena and by the impact of humans. Huge swaths of landscape can dramatically change overnight from flash floods and wildfires. Periodic events such as drought, wet seasons, insect

Delicate plants growing in a fragile habitat in Porphyry Basin near Silverton, Colorado
Michael Guidi

infestation, and the Earth's warming trend are all challenging to the inhabitants of the region. So is industry, tourism, and widespread development of the Rocky Mountain region.

This guidebook not only shares the story of the healing plants that occupy this region but promotes their use as medicine and even provides instruction on how to harvest them in the wild. Collecting plants in the wild for medicine and food is a joyful and rewarding experience that strengthens our bond with nature by encouraging a relationship with the plants that grow around us. The more we learn about these plants, the more we learn to respect them and nurture them. But we must take care of these plants and the environment they live in. As herbalists, foragers, hikers, and outdoor enthusiasts, we all have a responsibility to be stewards of the land, and protectors of the plants and animals that call this region home.

ETHICAL WILDCRAFTING GUIDELINES

Below you will find a list of ethical wildcrafting guidelines to keep in mind when walking the woods in search of medicinal plants for harvest.

1. **Know how to correctly identify plants.** Practice identifying plants by brushing up on basic botany and plant identification. Know that it takes practice, time, and repeated visits to master plant identification. Learn everything you can about the plants you are trying to harvest—their habitat, smell, and time of year they bloom. It is also helpful to learn look-alikes to avoid harvesting the wrong plant. Lastly, study the poisonous plants that live in the region where you are harvesting.

2. **Only harvest plants that are abundant.** Learn which plants grow profusely in the region in which you are collecting. Visit and hike several areas in your region and make a mental note of which plants you see growing in abundance. Lean toward harvesting plants that grow throughout the region rather than in a special or localized environment. Hike greater distances and gather small amounts along the way. Familiarize yourself with common weeds and invasive plants that hold nutritional and medicinal value. This category of plants can be harvested freely. If the plant seems sparse or rare, consider an alternative, or purchase at a local apothecary or online from an ethical source.

3. **Protect endangered plants.** Avoid harvesting rare and endangered plants altogether. Before harvesting in the wild, familiarize yourself with plants that are endangered in your region. Most endangered medicinal plants can be substituted with plants that are more common. For instance, the endangered *Astragalus humillimus* can be substituted with the more widespread *A. americanus* because they are quite similar medicinally.

4. **Take only what you need.** Have a plan before you harvest in the wild. Think about what remedies you would like to create before harvesting. Estimate how much plant material you will need for a remedy to ensure nothing is wasted.

5. **Bring proper tools.** Proper tools will ensure you harvest efficiently and avoid damage to the plant and surrounding environment. Pruners and a garden knife are essential tools for harvesting. Paper or plastic bags and labels are also helpful.

6. **Avoid polluted areas.** Avoid areas such as roadsides, public parks, lawns, and parking lots that may contain medicinal and edible plants; it is likely the plants in these areas contain pollutants. Natural areas including national forests and Bureau of Land Management (BLM) lands may look pristine and untouched, but it is possible they have been sprayed with herbicides and pesticides or contain pollutants from mining or nearby development. Some plants are considered bioaccumulators and may absorb harmful chemicals in polluted areas. Goldenrod, alfalfa, and yellow dock are examples of bioaccumulators.

7. **Practice stewardship.** Be a thoughtful and responsible visitor to the wilderness to ensure the land from which you are harvesting remains unaffected by your visit. Practice "leave no trace" by carrying out all trash or waste. Avoid stepping on delicate habitat whenever possible by staying on the trail. Respect wildlife by keeping your distance, avoid feeding animals, and minimize any stress to their environment.

8. **Thoughtfully harvest.** When harvesting a particular species of plant, only take 10 percent of the plant population in a given area. If cutting the plant, take only the top third to ensure that it will grow back healthy. When digging up roots, place any remaining roots back in the ground after harvest and replace dirt and leaves to make the area look natural. If a stream is nearby, or you have water on hand, offer some to the plant.

9. **Get permission.** Unless you are harvesting from your own land or garden, always obtain permission from landowners, written or verbal, before harvesting plants. State parks, BLM land, and other government-owned areas have strict laws in place meant to protect wildlife and plants that inhabit the region. National parks prohibit the collection of plants within their boundaries unless a permit is obtained. Most national forests require permission prior to harvesting. The US Forest Service has laws and regulations in place which can vary from district to district. Call or visit your local district and explain to them your plans for harvesting, learn how to obtain a permit, and stay updated on current rules that need to be followed.

Respect wildlife and enjoy from afar.
Jen Toews

These ethical guidelines are meant to teach us respect and thoughtfulness, and to live in harmony with the plants that live around us. Following these basic rules ensures that these plants are accessible for generations to come. Rather than thinking of these plants as a commodity, build a relationship with these healing herbs. When humans offer respect and care to the plants, this respect and care will be reciprocated.

ALTERNATIVES TO HARVESTING IN THE WILD

Wildcrafting can be a very rewarding experience for the forager, and in some cases, beneficial for the environment. Searching for and gathering plants in the wild can be easy, affordable, and may have a low carbon footprint. Not only are fresh, wild-gathered herbs arguably more potent, but gathering from the true source, Mother Nature, feels special. However, in many circumstances, foraging for plants in the wild may not be the best way to obtain plants for at-home use. Wildcrafting requires extensive knowledge about the plant including plant identification, specific habitat, and its peak time to harvest. In addition, time, navigation skills, and physical strength are required to access some of the rugged and pristine areas of the Rocky Mountains where these plants can be found. Thus, in some cases, it is best to leave the harvesting to the professionals.

Fortunately, local grocers, farmers' markets, and health food stores often carry an array of medicinal plants and remedies. Within a grocery store, it is common to see organic thyme, sage, and mint in the refrigerated herb section. In the produce aisle, nopales, aloe leaves, onions, garlic, ginger, and other plants used as traditional medicine are fresh, high quality, and relatively inexpensive. Many health food stores have a section of commercially prepared herbal remedies such as syrups, salves, and tinctures.

Many of the medicinal plants that are featured in this guidebook can be grown throughout much of the United States and Canada, especially in temperate areas in and around the Rocky Mountain region. Growing these medicinal plants in your home garden keeps cost low and reduces the chance of harvesting plants in nonorganic or polluted environments. Most importantly, remedies made from plants that we cared for and nurtured ourselves can be superior to commercial products.

Information for cultivating the medicinal plants listed in this text are included with the descriptions for those species that can be grown in gardens in the Rocky Mountain region and beyond. The USDA plant hardiness zones are based on average annual winter temperatures of a region. The zones help indicate which plants are likely to survive winters in specific areas of the United States. An updated map of the plant hardiness zones can be found at www.planthardiness .ars.usda.gov.

BASICS OF PLANT IDENTIFICATION

The practice of plant identification may take years, if not a lifetime to master, but it's well worth the effort. The Rocky Mountain region alone is home to thousands of species of plants, and to an untrained eye, identifying each of these plants can seem like a daunting task. But with a little curiosity, patience, and practice one can quickly learn how to identify the plants of any region. Plant identification is an important skill to have, especially if one is planning to forage or harvest these plants from the wild. The Rocky Mountain region is home to many healing and beneficial plants; however, it is also home to several species that can harm or even kill if improperly handled. Thus, knowing which plant you are about to eat or process into a medicinal remedy could become a matter of life and death. Setting fear aside, plant identification is a fun activity that is engaging to the hiker and creates an appreciative relationship between human and plant.

Plant identification may take a lifetime to master.
Jen Toews

Here are a few helpful tips to consider when you are out on the trail and learning to correctly identify a plant:

1. **Take a guidebook with you every time you hike.** Any regionally specific field guide with a dichotomous key will be a helpful tool. A dichotomous key

utilizes the unique characteristics of a plant (shape, color, number of petals, leaf shape) to help correctly identify an unfamiliar plant species. The key presents two choices to the reader, in a step-by-step basis, based on characteristics of the plant in question. Correctly selecting the right choice leads you to the next set of options, ultimately leading the reader to correct identificaton of the plant in question. Try identifying a new plant every time you hike. Take a photo of the plant and compare your identification with what you research on the internet or other plant identification books. Also read about the plants you already can properly identify and pay attention to the descriptions, familiarizing yourself with the language of plant identification.

2. **Know basic plant anatomy.** Acquaint yourself with the very basic structures and names of a plant, especially the anatomy of a flower and a leaf.

3. **Learn the plant families.** Flowering plants grouped into the same family often have similar characteristics. For example, plants in the rose family usually have flowers with five petals and sepals with numerous stamens. Mint family members are typically fragrant and have square stems. Plants in the carrot family have flowers with an umbel formation. Learn the basic characteristics of the plant families in your region to identify unknown plants more quickly.

4. **Study the plant using your senses.** Bring yourself closer to the plant to observe both large and subtle characteristics of the species. Notice tiny hairs, leaf patterns, and color, and count the petals or sepals. Gently touch the plant noticing the texture. Smell the flowers and leaves, noticing any hint of fragrance.

5. **Consider the surroundings.** Notice the habitat in which the plant you are studying is growing. Many plants have specific growing conditions and areas they prefer. Take note of elevation, the month in which it is blooming, and in what kind of environment it is growing. Considering these factors may help you arrive at a more decisive conclusion.

Next narrow down your list of possibilities by learning what type of plant it may be and studying the leaves and flowers. Below you will find some tips to help you identify plants while out on the trail. You can also find a glossary of plant terms in the back of this guidebook.

PLANT IDENTIFICATION TERMINOLOGY

Learning to identify the plants of the Rocky Mountains is an engaging and immersive practice, and an invaluable tool for a practicing herbalist. To know the plants that are growing in our magnificent and majestic mountains is to appreciate them. To state it simply, life as we know it would not exist without plants. Learn their names, observe their habitat, study their ethnobotanical importance. They all have a fascinating story to tell, and each plant plays a vital role in the health and longevity of the forests, grasslands, and deserts we love to hike in and explore.

The first step is to determine if the plant is a tree, shrub, vine; herbaceous perennial or annual; or a graminoid. Is the plant evergreen or deciduous? A monocot or a dicot?

Habit and Perennation

Perennial: plant that persists over many growing seasons

Annual: plant which performs its entire life cycle (seed to plant to seed) in one growing season

Tree: single-stemmed, woody plants greater than 10 meters in height

Shrub: usually a multistemmed woody plant less than 10 meters in height

Woody perennial: type of tree, shrub, or vine that does not die back in the winter, often with woody stems

Herbaceous perennial: plants that die to the ground each year, and go dormant during the winter

Evergreen: a plant that does not shed its leaves in the winter

Deciduous: a plant that sheds its leaves annually

Monocot: a plant that produces an embryo with one cotyledon (seed leaf)

Dicot: a plant that produces an embryo with two cotyledons

Leaf Identification

While plant identification by flower can be more reliable, leaves offer good clues when trying to identify a plant. This is especially true if a unique characteristic of the leaf can help set it apart from other closely related species. Plus, flowers are fleeting and may not be present on the plant at the time of identification. Start by identifying the leaf type and arrangement. Is it a simple leaf or compound? Some leaves are opposite one another on a stem, while others alternate in formation up the stem. Consider the shape of the leaf to help identify the plant. Some are thin like a blade, while others are round, lance-, or oval-shaped. Leaf margins, or the edges of the leaf, can be useful characteristics as well. Some plants have leaves with smooth edges, while others are jagged, lobed, or wavy. Other characteristics such as leaf attachment, leaf venation, color, and texture are important. Through the process of elimination it is possible to identify a plant simply through observing the leaves.

Flower Identification

The flowers often offer even more definitive clues to identifying a plant. If you find a plant in bloom, attempt to identify it by both leaf and flower. Keep in mind that some flowers are too small to observe with the naked eye or may vary morphologically within a species. However, being able to recognize some basic floral characteristics can lead you to a correct identification. Notice the color of the flower first as well as the overall size of the flower. The arrangement of the flower or flowers can be indicative of a particular plant family or genus. A cluster of flowers is called an inflorescence and there are multiple types of these flower arrangements that once learned will aid in identifying a plant's family or genus more quickly. The more features you can identify, the closer you are to a correct identification. How many petals are on the flower, or are they too numerous to count? Is the flower symmetrical or irregular?

Inflorescence Types:

Spike: flowers have no stalk (sessile); youngest flowers at the top
Raceme: each flower has a stalk (pedicelled); youngest flowers at the top
Panicle: raceme with a group of flowers, instead of just one on a stalk
Corymb: pedicels are differing lengths; flat or round top
Umbel: pedicels arising from a common point with a flat or convex top
Cyme: inflorescence where terminal flowers bloom first
Helicoid cyme: coiled inflorescence

Poisonous Plants

The Rocky Mountain region is home to several species of toxic plants that can result in injury, severe physiological reaction, or even death. These plants can look rather benign, often blending in with other plants, and some even resemble edible or medicinal species. Some are eye-catching or even appetizing to both humans and animals. Before foraging for consumption or medicine making, study these plants. Be cautious and know which plants you are harvesting and processing into medicine. Learn to identify their defining characteristics, their habitat, and how to spot them at all stages during the growing season. Keep in mind this brief list does not cover every toxic plant of the Rocky Mountain region.

Delphinium barbeyi
Mike Kintgen

WESTERN POISON IVY
Toxicodendron rydbergii

T. *rydbergii* can vary in color from green to red.
Jen Toews © Denver Botanic Gardens

Leaves with 3 ovate leaflets
Jen Toews © Denver Botanic Gardens

Family: ANACARDIACEAE/SUMAC

Similar plants: Poison ivy blends in well with many plants and foliage in the wilderness.

Warning: Coming into contact with poison ivy can cause severe dermatitis. Symptoms include hives, inflammation, blisters, and itchiness. There are reported cases of hospitalization of those who are severely allergic.

Season: Blooms May to July

Habitat and range: Open to shady sites in fertile, well-drained soil; plains to foothills; throughout much of the western United States

Description: Deciduous shrub with an erect or cascading growth habit. Leaves are alternate, divided into 3 ovate leaflets with a pointed tip 3–15 centimeters long. Undersides of leaves have visible veins, are glossy green but turn red in the fall. Flowers are white and in panicles; cup-shaped with 5 spreading petals. Fruits are white to green, in clusters, and are berries or drupes, 5–7 millimeters across.

Berries of western poison ivy
Jen Toews © Denver Botanic Gardens

POISON HEMLOCK
Conium maculatum

Conium maculatum in bloom
Cindy Newlander © Denver Botanic Gardens

Red or purple streaking is often present on lower stem.
Jen Toews © Denver Botanic Gardens

Family: APIACEAE/CARROT

Similar plants: Resembles many species within the carrot family including *Sium suave* (water parsnip), *Daucus carota* (Queen Anne's lace), and *Heracleum maximum* (cow parsnip)

Warning: Poison hemlock contains coniine, an extremely poisonous alkaloid. Just 300 milligrams of coniine, equivalent to 7 hemlock leaves, is enough to kill a human. Intoxication has also been reported in livestock and pets. Avoid inhaling and touching the plant, which can also cause severe illness.

Season: Blooms June to August

Habitat and range: Found along roadsides, meadows, and streambanks, often in moist soil throughout much of North America

Description: Herbaceous biennial flowering plant which can reach 3 meters in height. Plant emits a musty, unpleasant odor. Stems are hollow, smooth, and contain red or purple streaks at the lower half. Leaves are opposite and compound, divided 3–4 times, triangular in shape, hairless. Inflorescence consists of tiny white to green flowers that have 5 petals, up to 6 centimeters wide. Fruits are 2–3 millimeters wide, egg-shaped with 2 seeds.

WATER HEMLOCK
Cicuta maculata

Flowers of water hemlock
Marylyn Feaver

Leaves of water hemlock
Dawn Hall

Family: APIACEAE/CARROT

Similar plants: Looks similar to many species within the carrot family including *Sium suave* (water parsnip), *Daucus carota* (Queen Anne's lace), and *Heracleum maximum* (cow parsnip)

Warning: Water hemlock is considered one of North America's most toxic plants. All parts of the plant are highly toxic, especially the roots. Ingesting this plant can cause severe convulsions, vomiting, seizures, and death.

Season: Blooms June to August

Habitat and range: Found in moist meadows, ditches, or in standing water throughout most of North America

Description: Perennial herb growing to 1–1.5 meters tall with erect, hollow stems, sometimes with purple blotches at the base. Compound leaves are alternate, divided 1 to 3 times and divided again into 3s. Leaves are lance-shaped, toothed, and veins of the leaf terminate at the notch between the teeth. Flowers are white to green, in compound umbels with a flat top up to 10 centimeters across. Fruit is a pair of oval light brown seeds, up to 4 millimeters long.

MOUNTAIN DEATH CAMAS
Anticlea elegans

Anticlea elegans
Cindy Newlander © Denver Botanic Gardens

The closely related *Toxicoscordion paniculatum* (synonym *Zigadenus paniculatus*), which is found from plains to subalpine, is also toxic.
Jen Toews

Family: MELANTHIACEAE/FALSE HELLEBORE

Also called: *Zigadenus elegans*

Similar plants: Death camas can easily be mistaken for *Allium* species (wild onion), as their leaves look similar. One way to tell species of the 2 genera apart is by smell: While almost all species of *Allium* have an onion- or garlic-like scent, the bulbs and leaves of death camas lack an oniony scent. Additionally, confusion can occur between the Middle and Northern Rockies species *Camassia quamash*, common camas, which has an edible bulb harvested in the fall when the flowers are no longer present, and the toxic look-alike *Anticlea*. There are several poisonous species of *Anticlea* and closely related *Toxicoscordion* growing in the Rocky Mountain region, including *T. paniculatum*, which grows in semidesert and foothills, and *T. venenosum*, which grows in foothills and montane regions of the Rockies.

Warning: All parts of *A. elegans* and *T. paniculatum*—bulb, leaves, flowers, and seeds—are poisonous. Symptoms of poisoning include excess salivation, vomiting, weakness, and coma. Ingesting this plant can cause severe illness and occasionally death.

Season: Blooms June to August

Habitat and range: Moist, open sites and meadows; foothills to alpine, throughout the Rocky Mountain region and across the northern United States and Canada

Description: Herbaceous perennial with mostly basal, slender, and grasslike leaves. Leaves up to 30 centimeters long and 2 centimeters wide with smooth edges and parallel lines. Erect flower stalk forms a raceme with up to 50 whiteish-green flowers. Each flower has 6 egg-shaped petals, with green-yellow heart-shaped glands at bases, forming a ring around the center. Fruit is a 3-part, erect, oval-shaped cone 20 millimeters long.

MONKSHOOD
Aconitum spp.

Family: RANUNCULACEAE/BUTTERCUP

Similar plants: *Aconitum* species resemble many *Delphinium* species, which are also poisonous. *Aconitum* leaves may be mistaken for geranium leaves or the leaves of certain mallows.

Warning: All parts of *Aconitum* contain the poisonous and deadly alkaloid aconitine. Avoid consuming or touching this plant.

Season: Blooms June to August

Habitat and range: Found in moist hillsides and meadows, open or shaded; from foothills to subalpine; southwestern, central, and northeastern United States and throughout Canada

Description: Herbaceous perennial with hollow stems that reach 120 centimeters tall. Leaves are alternate and palmate with 3–5 lobes, 5–15 centimeters wide; no stip-

Monkshood (*Aconitum columbianum*) in bloom
Cindy Newlander © Denver Botanic Gardens

ules. Flowers are blueish purple, usually clustered; 4 centimeters high and 2 centimeters wide, each flower has 5 sepals, the upper form a hood-like structure over the others; 5 petals and numerous stamens. Fruits are erect pods, 2 centimeters long, containing seeds.

BANEBERRY
Actaea rubra

Family: RANUNCULACEAE/BUTTERCUP

Also called: Red cohosh, snakeberry

Similar plants: Leaves superficially resemble sweet cicely and raspberry, and the fruit looks enticing, similar to rosehips or currant.

Warning: Ingestion of this plant can cause diarrhea, stomach cramps, and vomiting.

Season: Blooms May to July

Habitat and range: This species inhabits moist and shady sites from foothills to montane. It is found throughout the southwestern and northeastern United States and throughout Canada.

Description: Perennial herb with erect stems growing to 100 centimeters tall. Leaves compound, alternate, 2–3 times divided, and usually in 3s. Leaves are coarsely toothed and

The fruit of *A. rubra* is enticing, but poisonous.
Cindy Newlander © Denver Botanic Gardens

A. rubra in bloom
Jen Toews

lobed and 3–10 centimeters long. Flowers are white with 5–10 petals and up to 5 sepals. Many flowers form a raceme. Fruits are red, round, and shiny and 1 centimeter across.

LARKSPUR
Delphinium spp.

Family: RANUNCULACEAE/BUTTERCUP

Similar plants: Leaves of delphinium look similar to some geranium species, and the flowers are similar to monkshood (*Aconitum*), which is another poisonous plant.

Warning: All parts of the *Delphinium* plant are extremely toxic and can be fatal. Avoid contact with *Delphinium* which can cause a severe rash.

Season: Blooms May to July

Habitat and range: Found in open or wooded sites from plains to subalpine. *Delphinium* grows throughout the United States and Canada.

Description: Perennial herb growing to 50 centimeters tall. Leaves, 2–6 centimeters

Derived from the Latin word *delphinus*, which translates to dolphin, the flower buds of delphiniums resemble dolphins.
Mike Kintgen © Denver Botanic Gardens

wide, are mostly basal, palmate with deep lobes and toothed margins. Deep purple flowers in racemes or clusters are 4 centimeters wide and 3 centimeters long with 5 sepals which fuse into a spur, and 4 inconspicuous petals. Fruits form hairy erect pods with spreading tips.

Medicinal Plants

Willow and wildflowers growing in Maroon Bells–Snowmass Wilderness, Colorado
Michael Guidi

ADOXACEAE/MOSCHATEL FAMILY

Woody and herbaceous flowering plants with showy flowers, opposite toothed leaves, and fleshy drupes

Sambucus cerulea
Mike Kintgen

ELDER
Sambucus cerulea

Sambucus cerulea
Mike Kintgen © Denver Botanic Gardens

Sambucus racemosa var. *microbotrys* with bright red fruit in midsummer
Mike Kintgen

Also called: Blue elderberry, Flor Sauco, *S. nigra* ssp. *cerulea*

Related species: *S. canadensis, S. racemosa*

Parts used: Flower, fruit

Cautions: All varieties of elderberries are likely to cause digestive irritation when consumed raw; however any toxins present in the fruit are destroyed by cooking.

Season: Blooms April to June. Harvest flowers at peak bloom. Harvest fruits late summer, when they are dark purple and tender to the touch.

Habitat and range: Grows on rocky slopes and near rivers from the foothills to montane in western North America

Description: Deciduous shrub or small tree reaching 10 meters in height and width. Leaves are opposite, pinnately compound, leaflets up to 15 centimeters long and 3–5 centimeters wide, lanceolate, serrate. Flowers yellowish to white, with 5 lobes 6 millimeters wide, in many branched, flat clusters. Berries are purplish black, and 6 millimeters across.

Constituents: Flavonoids, mucilaginous polysaccharides, tannins, volatile oil, minerals, triterpenes

Medicinal actions: Diaphoretic, expectorant, diuretic, refrigerant, laxative, demulcent, emollient

Cultivation: *S. cerulea, S. nigra*, and other species of elder can grow in a variety of soil types from sandy to clay. Although they prefer moist soil, they can tolerate drier soils once established. Plant in a sunny location for best growth and bloom, or in part shade. Zones 4–8.

Nearly every mountainous region or forest of the Rocky Mountains is home to an elder species. *Sambucus racemosa* var. *microbotrys* (red and yellow berries), *S. racemosa* var. *melanocarpa* (black and purple berries), and *S. cerulea* (blueish-purple berries) mingle within aspen stands and grow alongside rivers throughout the region. While all ripe elderberries are considered medicinal and edible, the black and blue varieties are more commonly consumed and provide a higher concentration of medicinal potency than the red variety. Elder has proven extremely important for Native Americans as a source of food, medicine, and wood to make a variety of goods including musical instruments. Native Americans use almost all parts of the elder shrub to treat various ailments including fever, pain, swelling, and diarrhea.

The flowers make a delicious floral tea, which, when served hot, is a diaphoretic capable of opening pores of the skin and cooling the body during feverish states. In addition to breaking fever, elder flower has laxative, anti-inflammatory, antiseptic, and antiviral properties which provide protection and relief from illness. In fact, an age-old herbal remedy for cold or flu is equal parts elder flower, peppermint leaf, and yarrow flower blend served as a warm beverage. The high flavonoid content of elder flower plays a key role to its healing powers. The flavonoid quercetin, found in elder flower, reduces cholesterol, and may help reduce oxidative stress on skin, blood vessels, and joints. Elder flower softens skin, tightens pores, and cleanses gently, yet effectively. For soft, clear skin, consider making skin oils, toners, and serums using elder flower. Elder flower is the main herb used in many liqueurs, including St. Germaine, and is also used in syrups, sodas, and candies.

The drupes of *Sambucus*, commonly known as elderberries, are prized for their high antioxidant content and their use as an immune booster and antiviral. Many medical studies have concluded that elderberries are effective in preventing and treating colds and flus. Taking high doses of elderberry syrup or tincture may strengthen the immune system and prevent the flu virus from invading the body. Medical research also suggests that consumption of cooked elderberries while ill with the cold or flu may help shorten the duration of the illness and help the body convalesce quicker. Once an obscure folk remedy, elderberry syrup is now commonly found in pharmacies and grocery stores around the world.

Fresh Elderberry Syrup

Make this remedy in September, when elderberries are fresh. This syrup is great to keep on hand during cold and flu season. Add to soda water for a refreshing beverage or turn into salad dressing with vinegar. If using dried berries, rehydrate berries by heating 2 cups of water for every 1 cup of dried berries. Reduce liquid until desired consistency is reached.

Ingredients:

1 cup fresh elderberries (stems removed)
1 cup water
1 cup honey
1 ounce gin or vodka

Instructions:

Place berries in a cooking pot. Pour 1 cup water into the pan. Bring berries and water to a boil, reduce heat, then gently simmer for 20 minutes. Mash with a large flat spoon to extract as much juice as possible. Use a muslin cloth to strain the juice into a mason jar. Measure the volume of juice and add an equal amount of honey (for every cup of juice add a cup of honey). Stir well and seal. To prevent spoilage, add 1 ounce of gin or vodka for every 8 ounces of syrup. Label and store in the refrigerator for 3 to 6 months, or place in the freezer until ready to consume.

AMARANTHACEAE/AMARANTH FAMILY

Both annual and perennial herbs and subshrubs with simple, usually alternate leaves

Chenopodium sp.
Jen Toews

LAMB'S QUARTERS
Chenopodium album

Also called: Goosefoot
Related species: *C. atrovirens, C. berlandieri, C. fremontii*
Parts used: Leaf
Cautions: None known
Season: Blooms July to September. Harvest leaves in spring when they are most tender.
Habitat and range: Grows in disturbed soil and cultivated sites and waste sites, from plains to montane. Grows throughout the United States.
Description: Fast-growing, several-stemmed annual; can reach 3 meters tall. Leaves are 3–10 centimeters long, dusty green, alternate, diamond-shaped, and irregularly lobed. Small flower spikes are green, in dense clusters, and with no petals and 5 sepals. Round, disc-shaped seeds are shiny black or dark green and covered in a white, papery sheath.

Chenopodium album
Jen Toews

Constituents: Phenols, tannins, oxalates, flavonoids, vitamins A and C, iron, phosphorus
Medicinal actions: Nutritive, hepatoprotective, diuretic, alterative
Cultivation: Due to the weedy nature of *Chenopodium album*, consider growing *C. berlandieri* instead. In the spring, spread seeds on soil surface and gently rake in. Water thoroughly, keeping the soil moist, until seeds have sprouted. Thin out seedlings to encourage more growth. This plant thrives in a wide variety of soil types and climates. Zones 3–10

For thousands of years, humans have been cultivating and consuming *Chenopodium* for its nutritional and medicinal properties. Lamb's quarters seeds contain high amounts of amino acids and minerals and are an excellent source of fiber. One lamb's quarters plant can produce up to 70,000 seeds. These seeds can be harvested, washed, dried, and ground into flour for cakes and breads, much like quinoa and amaranth. Whole seeds can be added to soups and stews, made into porridge, or sprouted for salads.

Lamb's quarters is a very nutritious plant: The leaves are an excellent source of vitamins A, B, and C and contain the minerals iron, calcium, phosphorus, and zinc. While lamb's quarters can be eaten raw, cook these greens for better assimilation of nutrients in the body. Cooking and processing will also degrade the oxalates in the leaf, which can be irritating if eaten in large amounts. Much like kale or spinach, lamb's quarters works well when cooked in fat, steamed, or added to soups, stews, and salads. *Chenopodium* has been used medicinally for centuries. Often, you will see *Chenopodium album* listed as a "blood purifier" in old herbals and ethnobotanical books. This is most likely due to its high nutritional value and diuretic properties, rather than its ability to clean blood. Lamb's quarters' leaves have anti-inflammatory properties, and a tea has been used to treat gout, rheumatic pains, and eczema. Leaves can also be wilted in hot water and laid on wounds, burns, and insect stings much like a cast. This will soothe the affected area.

Lamb's Quarters Spread

Use arugula, spinach, or parsley in place of lamb's quarters.

Ingredients:

2 cloves garlic, peeled
1 small red or white onion, peeled
2 cups lamb's quarters leaves
1 ripe avocado, peeled and pitted
½ cup toasted nuts
⅓ cup pitted Kalamata olives
2 tablespoons mellow (light-colored) miso
1 tablespoon chili paste or 1 teaspoon cayenne pepper, or to taste

Instructions:

Chop garlic, onion, lamb's quarters leaves, avocado, nuts, and olives. Add miso and seasoning and mix by hand or in a food processor. Lamb's quarters spread will keep, tightly covered, in the refrigerator for 5 to 7 days.

Makes 2 ½ cups

AMARYLLIDACEAE/AMARYLLIS FAMILY

Perennial and bulbous flowering plants with 3 to 6 petals and usually linear leaves

Allium geyeri
Mike Kintgen

WILD ONION
Allium cernuum

Related species: *A. geyeri, A. textile*

Parts used: Bulb, leaf, flower

Cautions: Alliums look very similar to the poisonous plant *Anticlea elegans* (mountain death camas). Wild onion leaves are hollow, and death camas leaves are not. The flower stem of death camas terminates in a raceme of green, white, or sometimes pink flowers. Wild onion has a strong onion smell, and umbel-like flower. While it's easy to differentiate between the 2 plants when in flower, it may be difficult when both species are not blooming. Always use caution when harvesting in the wild.

Allium cernuum in cultivation
Jen Toews

Season: Blooms June to August. Harvest the bulb or aerial parts when in full bloom.

Habitat and range: Wild onions prefer sunny locations including open woods and dry meadows and are commonly found from plains to alpine throughout the Rocky Mountains and also in central and eastern North America.

Description: *Allium* are perennial herbs with slender leafless stems to 50 centimeters, which grow from a singular, egg-shaped bulb. Leaves are grasslike, flat, and some-what sparse. Flowers, in umbels, are usually

The flowers of *Allium cernuum* nod.
Jen Toews

white to purple, and have 3 petals, 3 sepals, 1 style, 6 stamens, and yellow anthers. Cutting or crushing any part of the plant will produce an unmistakable, onion-like smell.

Constituents: Quercetin, sulphur compounds, alliins, carbohydrates

Medicinal actions: Nutritive, antibacterial, anti-inflammatory, wound healing, diuretic, antioxidant

Cultivation: Grow *Allium cernuum* in full sun or part shade in well-drained soil or containers. Sow seeds in fall or plant seedlings in spring, keeping them moist until established. Divide plants every few years. Zones 3–8

Wild onions are common in the Rocky Mountain region and throughout much of the United States. The wild onion species, *A. cernuum*, that grows profusely in the Rocky Mountains makes an excellent trail snack or a great addition to backcountry camping meals. All parts of the plant are edible including the bulb and flowers. Much like garlic and the common onion found in local grocery stores, nodding onion has many medicinal benefits. Onions contain a powerful flavonoid called quercetin, a pigment found in many fruits and vegetables. Quercetin is an extremely potent antioxidant which prevents and slows cellular damage, cancer, and degenerative diseases in the body. Recent medical studies have also shown quercetin may help lower blood cholesterol. A 2019 study in the *Asia Pacific Journal of Clinical Oncology* compared 833 people with colorectal cancer with 833 people who did not have the disease. The researchers found that the risk of colorectal cancer was 79 percent lower in those who regularly consumed *Allium* vegetables, such as onions. Although experts do not fully understand the exact mechanism by which some compounds in onions inhibit cancer, some hypothesize that onions inhibit tumor growth and cell mutation.

Onion also contains strong antibacterial and anti-inflammatory properties. During a bout with an illness such as cold or flu, inflammation is rampant and mucus builds in the body. The compounds present in onions help reduce inflammation and can even thin mucus in the lungs, allowing it to be expelled from the body when we cough. Hence, onion is an expectorant. With that in mind, consider making a readily available onion cough syrup for the upcoming winter. This simple remedy can keep inflammation down and bacteria at bay.

Locating *Allium* during its growing season is not difficult but keep its sparse and slight stature in mind. The wild onions found in our region are typically smaller in size and the bulb of the plant may only be the size of a dime or quarter. This means that harvesting large quantities in the wild is labor intensive. The best way to utilize this plant is to just eat it. There is something to be said about picking a few leaves, or tender flower heads of the nodding onion, and savoring them on a hike. The pleasant, but pungent garlic and onion notes linger in the mouth for the next mile. Gather a small bundle of onion leaves, chop them up, and add to a camping dinner, or sauté in oil with cutthroat trout. Like Hippocrates states: "Let food be thy medicine and medicine be thy food." In the beginning stages of a budding herbalist, it is common to want to tincture everything, or turn our whole garden into a salve, because it is exciting. But it's important to remember that food is medicine as well.

Wild Onion Oil

Ingredients:

½ cup wild onion bulbs, cleaned
½ cup olive oil

Instructions:

1. After washing, pat the bulbs dry. Excess water mixed with oil may encourage mold growth.
2. Place bulbs in a jar and cover with olive oil. Tightly cover the jar and store in the refrigerator for up to 2 weeks, shaking daily to encourage maceration.
3. Strain out the solids and use the wild onion oil in any recipe that calls for oil. Store the onion oil in a jar in the refrigerator for up to 6 weeks.

Yield: ½ cup

Onion Cough Syrup

If wild onions are scarce, store-bought onions or even garlic cloves would be an appropriate substitution.

Ingredients:

1 large onion
1 cup white or brown sugar

Instructions:

Peel the onion and slice thinly into ½-inch rounds. Place one layer of onion in a mason jar and sprinkle ½ tablespoon of sugar on top. Add another layer of onion and sprinkle another ½ tablespoon of sugar on top. Continue layering onion and sugar until all of the onion is in the jar. Seal and label the jar, then let it sit at room temperature for 8 hours. Syrup will form naturally. Pour out syrup and use as a cough suppressant and expectorant. Discard or refrigerate after use.

ANACARDIACEAE/SUMAC FAMILY

Evergreen and deciduous trees, shrubs and vines, usually dioecious, with compound leaves and fleshy drupes

Rhus glabra is known for its stunning fall color.
Mike Kintgen

SKUNKBUSH SUMAC
Rhus trilobata

Also called: *R. aromatica* var. *trilobata*, sour berry, 3-leaf sumac

Related species: *R. glabra, R. typhina*

Parts used: Fruit, occasionally bark, leaf, root

Cautions: Sap may cause skin irritation.

Rhus trilobata
Gary Waggoner © Denver Botanic Gardens

Rhus trilobata in fruit
Blake Burger

Season: Blooms April to July; harvest fruits from late summer into the fall

Habitat and range: Found in the plains and foothills in canyons, dry slopes, and near streams throughout the Rocky Mountain region; native throughout the western United States, west of the Missouri River

Description: Deciduous shrub to 2 meters tall. Leaves are compound, alternate, and divided into 3 lobed leaflets. Leaves have a waxy coating, a skunky odor when crushed, and turn bright red and orange in the fall. Numerous small, cream-colored flowers grow near the tips of branches. Reddish-orange fruits are hairy and sticky, sometimes with a citruslike aroma.

Constituents: Tannins, volatile oil, glycoside, phenolic acids, flavonoids, triterpenes

Medicinal actions: Astringent, anti-inflammatory, diuretic, antimicrobial

Cultivation: Grows in well-drained, fertile soil in full sun. This variety grows well in xeric gardens, tolerating periods of drought. Sumac offers colorful fall foliage, food for wildlife, and attracts pollinators. Zones 4–8

Rhus trilobata is one of about 50 species in the *Rhus* (sumac) genus. The word sumac, which has origins in French, Latin, and Arabic, refers to the color red. In fact, several species of *Rhus* are utilized to make yellow, red, and brown dyes. Perhaps the most popular use, however, is as a culinary spice. In many regions of the world, the dried drupes (fruits) are ground up and used as a spice. The sumacs of the Great Plains and Rocky Mountain regions, specifically *Rhus trilobata*, hold ethnobotanical significance because of their importance for dye, cosmetics, food, and medicine. The leaves of sumac are high in tannins, and thus make a great natural dye, coloring fabrics a blackish brown. The twigs yield a yellow dye and the fruits a pinkish-red color. Medicinally, the leaves and inner bark were traditionally employed as a cold remedy, a practice uncommon in modern herbalism. The tannic leaves and twigs make an astringent decoction that can be applied to minor irritations to cleanse and soothe. The astringent leaves are also an effective hemostatic, helping to stop blood flow from cuts and wounds.

Native Americans have traditionally used the drupes as an analgesic, digestive aid, and for their sour astringent taste. A powdered form of the drupes was once a remedy for pox, stopping itch and easing pain. A tea of the drupes has been used to treat upset stomach and diarrhea that accompany the stomach flu. The ripened berries, which are tart, make a delicious trail snack, in small quantities. For a refreshing and tart beverage similar to lemonade, steep the fruits in cold water for 20–30 minutes. Brewing the drupes in hot water will pull out more tannins, creating a more astringent, medicinal beverage.

APIACEAE/CARROT FAMILY

Mostly annual, biennial, or perennial herbs with alternate leaves without stipules; flowers in compound umbels

Lomatium laevigatum, a rare species of the Pacific Northwest, displays the rounded, compound flower umbels that are characteristic of the carrot family.
Mike Kintgen

GRAY'S ANGELICA
Angelica grayi

Related species: *Angelica archangelica*

Parts used: Root, stem, seed

Cautions: Many species of the carrot family have similar physical characteristics and are highly toxic. For example, one could easily mistake the poisonous water hemlock for angelica.

Season: Blooms June to August. Harvest young stems in spring or early summer. Root should be harvested in the fall.

Habitat and range: Commonly found in meadows and rocky areas in the montane, subalpine, and alpine regions of the Southern Rockies from Wyoming to New Mexico

Description: *Angelica grayi* is an herbaceous perennial from 15 to 60 centimeters tall. The thick, grooved flower stalk is hollow and the main stem is sheathed at the base. Leaves, often widely spaced along the stem, are alternate and pinnate, with prominent veins and serrated edges. Inflorescence a spherical umbel, with up to 20 umbellules of numerous white flowers. Flowers have a green center, white petals, and several protruding stamens. Fruit a double, egg-shaped seed that is flat in the center and convex on the exterior.

Constituents: Volatile oil, sugars, essential oil, bitter principles, flavonoids, and sterols

Medicinal action: Digestive aid, sedative, carminative, diuretic, diaphoretic, tonic, and expectorant

Cultivation: *A. grayi* prefers moist, slightly alkaline soil, and sun to part shade. In hotter climates, more shade is best. Zones 3–10

Angelica grayi with fruit starting to form
Mike Kintgen © Denver Botanic Gardens

There are over 50 species of *Angelica* growing throughout the temperate Northern Hemisphere. Interestingly, regardless of the region in which *Angelica* is growing, humans revere it as a source of food, for spiritual practices, and for medicine. For example, in Iceland and the Faroe Islands, Indigenous peoples consider their native *Angelica* species a vegetable. The young leaves are a nutritious green, and the stems can be cooked in stews or candied. The Samis, Indigenous people inhabiting what is now Sweden, Norway, and Finland, use *A. archangelica* and other herbs to preserve reindeer milk. This mixture of herbs and berries, called gompa, is cooked into a porridge and mixed with reindeer milk.

There is also historical documentation of *Angelica archangelica* being used as protection against evil spirits,

Angelica grayi in flower
Jen Toews

hexes, and to promote good fortune. According to folk legends, the archangel Michael appeared in the dream of an influential monk and told the monk of the powers of angelica. This premonition led to the idea of using angelica root as a cure for the plague that ravaged Europe during medieval times.

Due to its complex assortment of constituents, *Angelica* has also been used to treat many ailments. It can remove heat and irritability in the body, thus promoting a more calm and balanced state. As a diuretic, it helps to move fluid through the body by increasing urination. As a diaphoretic, angelica opens pores and sebaceous glands to cool the body. As a sedative, it calms the mind. Herbalist Michael Moore recommends angelica root tea for feverish irritability or "hot" illnesses ranging from IBS to fevers and even arthritis. As a circulatory system tonic, angelica may help reduce blood pressure and body temperature. Finally, angelica can be used to regulate menstruation and to treat cramping.

Carminative Tea

A cup of this tea will ease the stomach after a big meal, helping to ease bloating and prevent discomfort from gas. This simple recipe can be multiplied by any amount and stored in a mason jar for easy preparation.

Ingredients:

1 teaspoon peppermint leaves
1 teaspoon angelica root
1 teaspoon fennel seeds
12 ounces boiling water

Instructions:

Combine these 3 herbs in a mason jar and add 12 ounces of boiling water. Cover the jar and steep for at least 5 minutes. Strain and enjoy. A second and third brew is possible by boiling more water and adding to the herbs in the mason jar. Drink a cup of this simple and delicious tea after a meal to relieve indigestion.

OSHA
Ligusticum porteri

Also called: Chuchupate, Colorado cough root, Porter's lovage
Related species: *L. filicinum, L. tenuifolium*
Parts used: Root

Ligusticum porteri
Mike Kintgen

Osha root
Blake Burger

Cautions: Plants in the family Apiaceae are easily confused and require positive identification before harvesting. Osha looks remarkably similar to poison hemlock and water hemlock, which are extremely toxic.

Season: Blooms June to August. Harvest root in the fall, after first frost.

Habitat and range: Found in aspen forests, open meadows, and on wet slopes in montane to subalpine from Montana to New Mexico and Nevada as well as northern Mexico

Description: Perennial herb to 1 meter tall with umbellate flowers, fernlike foliage, and a dark brown, hairy root. Stems are hollow and leaves are primarily basal and finely divided. Bases of stems, where attached to root crowns, have a reddish tint. White flowers are 2–5 millimeters across with 5 petals and are grouped in flat-topped compound umbels. Red fruits are ribbed, with rounded heads, and resemble fennel seeds.

Constituents: Essential oils, coumarins, polyacetylenes, phenolic acid

Medicinal actions: Antispasmodic, expectorant, anti-inflammatory, bitter tonic, antibacterial

Cultivation: Osha prefers nutrient-rich, well-drained soil. Plant in part shade, avoiding intense afternoon sun, or excessively dry soil. This species can be very challenging to cultivate. Zones 3–6

Osha root is used extensively by Indigenous cultures of North America as a medicinal herb, ceremonial plant, and as food. Also known as bear medicine, several Native American cultures learned of osha's nutritional and medicinal properties by observing bears using this plant in the wild. After a long hibernation, bears seek out osha's nutritious and spicy root to fatten up and encourage circulation. In Alaska, Kodiak bears chew on roots of a similar species of osha, then place the root particles mixed with saliva on infected wounds. Believing that bears gifted this root to humans, many Native American cultures of the West treasure this herb.

Osha is well respected by modern herbalists as a strong expectorant and lung tonic, appropriate for illnesses affecting the respiratory system including bronchitis, laryngitis, and pneumonia. Osha contains high amounts of antioxidants, reducing inflammation and oxidative damage. This herb thins mucus, enabling coughs to be more productive. As a strong antiviral, osha provides protection from a virus that has just begun to attack the body. Osha even shows promise in treating herpes and HIV. Osha boosts immune function in the body, helping to fight off the infection completely or reducing the severity and duration of the illness. Other uses for the root medicine include indigestion, sore throat, skin abrasions, and superficial infections.

Osha root is also effective in treating altitude sickness. A small dose of osha root tincture, or root added to tea, is recommended for those traveling from sea level to high elevations. Headache, shortness of breath, nausea, or other symptoms that accompany altitude sickness are alleviated by osha root. There is also promise in athletes using osha root to increase lung and heart function while engaging in cardiac activities.

Osha root can be purchased through many online sources: Look for roots that have been wildcrafted, ethically and responsibly harvested. Osha grows plentifully in the wild, but be absolutely certain it is not poison hemlock, *Conium maculatum,* or water hemlock, *Cicuta maculata.* To obtain a confident identification, keep a few basics in mind. Osha thrives in moist, nutrient-rich soil alongside spruce and aspen at high elevations. Poison hemlock grows at much lower elevations and often shows purple splotches on the stem. Water hemlock grows as high as osha but prefers bodies of water, such as a stream. Osha has an unmistakable scent of spicy celery, while poison and water hemlocks have a rank scent. Both *Cicuta maculata* and *Conium maculatum* have a hairless root, while osha root is brown and hairy with yellow tinted flesh when peeled.

To extract the powerful medicine of osha, make a tea or a tincture. If the root is harvested fresh, cut into small pieces before drying as it may be difficult to cut once it has hardened. Once harvested, osha root can be dried in the sun, or dried slowly anywhere with good air flow and low humidity. Fresh osha root can be irritating to the mouth, so dry before ingesting. Dried osha root can be stored for years. When making osha root tea, rather than discarding the valuable root after one use, allow the root to dry after boiling in water and use repeatedly.

Osha Tincture

Osha tincture is an invaluable respiratory remedy that should be considered a staple in your herbal medicine cabinet.

Ingredients:

4 ounces fresh osha root
16 ounces 100 proof vodka

Instructions:

Place the osha root into a pint or quart mason jar and submerge with vodka. Shake daily for 3 to 4 weeks and store in a dark place. Strain if desired, or keep root submerged in vodka.

SWEET CICELY
Osmorhiza occidentalis

Also called: Mountain sweet cicely, sweet root
Related species: *O. berteroi, O. longistylis*
Parts used: Root, leaf, seed
Cautions: None known
Season: Blooms April to June. Harvest leaves in spring or early summer. Seeds can be harvested from summer into the fall.
Habitat and range: Found in moist, shady forests and slopes near creeks in submontane and montane throughout northwestern North America to southern Colorado and Utah

Osmorhiza occidentalis's delicate flowers will be replaced by dark-colored seedpods.
Mike Kintgen

Description: Aromatic perennial from 30 to 100 centimeters tall with thick taproot and 1–3 stems; grows in clusters in moist forests and singly in dry forests. Leaves, 3–6 centimeters long, are twice divided into 3 leaflets, have serrated margins, slightly hairy surfaces, and a pointed tip. Inconspicuous flowers are greenish white and grow in umbels. Dark, bristly seeds (12–23 mm) are long, slender, and glossy and resemble dill or fennel. Sweet cicely root can grow quite substantially in older plants, reaching the size of a large carrot or bigger.
Constituents: Volatile oils, flavonoids
Medicinal actions: Digestive, aromatic, antiseptic, carminative, expectorant
Cultivation: Prefers moist, loamy soil and part shade, especially during the afternoon. Keep soil moist if direct sowing. Zones 5–9

Osmorhiza depauperata has wispy flowers and elongated club-like fruit.
Mike Kintgen

The whole plant, including the root, leaves, and seeds, is edible and medicinal. This spicy aromatic herb smells like anise, licorice, or root beer, and contains some of the same properties as *Glycyrrhiza lepidota* (licorice root). Young leaves, which can be used much like spinach, are a delicious and nutritious addition to salads, stews, or pesto. A tea can be made from fresh or dried leaves. In fact, the leaves dry well and can be stored for up to a year. The anise flavor within the seeds pleasantly lingers after being chewed.

The uses for sweet cicely root by Indigenous peoples of the Rocky Mountain region and North America are extensive. Shoshoni use the root as an analgesic by placing small pieces in the nostrils to relieve headaches. Shoshoni medicine recommends an infusion of the root to regulate menstruation, or for use as a cough syrup to combat cold and flu. Blackfoot mix this root with other medicinal plants to treat infant colds and coughs. Sweet cicely root can be administered to both boost immunity and to convalesce.

As an antiseptic, a decoction of the root helps complications caused by candidiasis, an excessive buildup of the yeast *Candida* that can lead to fatigue, sinus infections, genital and urinary tract infections, and skin and nail fungus. A root decoction can be applied as a soak, douche, or enema to reduce localized buildup of yeast and fungus. In addition to preventing yeast and fungus, this root also makes a great antiseptic wash for abrasions, scrapes, and cuts on the skin. Sweet cicely root can also be tinctured in brandy, vodka, or other high proof spirits.

Older herbal publications classify the root and leaves of *Osmorhiza occidentalis* as a tonic or adaptogen, especially for the elderly. Perhaps this is due to the invigorating essential oils found throughout the plant, or because of the presence of glycyrrhizin, the compound found in licorice root, which has adaptogenic properties. For example, the warming root fortifies the blood, builds strength, and helps improve digestion. Due to the presence of iron in the root, a decoction of the root was once commonly prescribed for anemic adolescent girls or adults. Finally, the root was also dried and burned as incense to enhance mood and cleanse the spirit.

Sweet Cicely Root Syrup

This syrup can be used as a cough syrup, mixer for cocktails, and to build strength after an illness.

Ingredients:

1 cup sugar or honey
¾ cup water
1 cup sweet cicely root, diced

Instructions:

Over medium heat, add sugar to water and stir constantly until the sugar is dissolved. Add cicely root to the syrup and bring to a light boil, reduce heat, cover, and simmer for 15 minutes. Turn off heat and let the mixture sit for 1 hour. Strain and store in a mason jar in a cool, dark place.

BLACK SNAKEROOT
Sanicula marilandica

Also called: American sanicle
Parts used: Root
Cautions: None known
Season: Blooms in June. Harvest the root in the fall after the first frost.
Habitat and range: Prefers moist, wooded sites with rich soil. Commonly found from the plains to foothills throughout much of Canada and the United States.
Description: Perennial with a single erect stem growing to 120 centimeters tall. Roots are fibrous and aromatic. Stem is reddish and furrowed. Leaves, which are mainly basal and palmately divided into 5 or 7 leaflets, are 5–15 centimeters wide, sharply toothed, and glossy green above and paler underneath. Flowers are greenish white, tiny, and in umbels of 15–25 flowers. Fruits are egg-shaped, 4–6 millimeters long, and with hooked bristles.
Constituents: Essential oils, tannins, resin
Medicinal actions: Astringent, antibacterial, analgesic, nervine, sedative, febrifuge, expectorant
Cultivation: *Sanicula* prefers part shade to shade. Although it tolerates a wide variety of soils, *Sanicula* prefers moist, well-draining soils. Zones 3–9

Sanicula marilandica in flower
Pat Deacon

Much of the information and evidence of snakeroot's healing capabilities stem from old European herbals and Native American medicine. Early European settlers of North America sought out *Sanicula* as a snakebite remedy (hence the common name snakeroot), crushing up the roots and applying as a poultice to draw out and neutralize the venom. The tannins found in the root are a valuable astringent, once widely used to treat "lax of the belly," or diarrhea. *Sanicula* can be employed for many types of wounds, ulcers, hemorrhages, and hemorrhoids to prevent infection and promote healing.

Known for its versatility, Native Americans trust snakeroot for reducing inflammation both topically and internally. In fact, snakeroot was considered a panacea, capable of healing all sorts of diseases and health issues. For instance, due to antibacterial properties of snakeroot, a decoction of the root is used as gargle for a sore throat, or that same decoction is prescribed as a wash to heal skin inflammation or drank as a tea to ease symptoms of gonorrhea. Some historical records suggest the use of *Sanicula* root as a treatment for cancer. This herb played an important role in healing St. Anthony's fire or erysipelas, a bacterial infection of the skin that causes spasms, diarrhea, and gangrenous tissues, which can lead to death. The root was an effective antibacterial and anti-inflammatory for this specific disease. First Nations such as the Micmac and Algonquin used the root as an analgesic. Besides treating sore throats, the root offers relief for sore muscles, pain and discomfort of the lungs and chest, as well as pain caused by sores and wounds.

Sanicula Root Gargle

For sore throat and discomfort, use this decoction as a gargle as often as needed. *Sanicula* decoction can be stored in the refrigerator for up to 3 days.

Ingredients:

3–5 ounces fresh root chopped
32 ounces water
3 tablespoons honey

Instructions:

Place fresh root in a saucepan, then add water. Bring the mixture to a boil, reduce heat, and simmer uncovered until the water is reduced by half. Turn off heat and strain decoction into a mason jar. Add honey and stir until blended.

APOCYNACEAE/DOGBANE FAMILY

Annual and perennial plants with simple leaves, radial flowers. Most plants exude a milky sap when injured.

Asclepias speciosa
Mike Kintgen

BUTTERFLY WEED
Asclepias tuberosa

Also called: Butterfly milkweed, common milkweed, pleurisy root
Related species: *A. incarnata, A. speciosa*
Parts used: Root
Cautions: A large dose of pleurisy root may cause nausea and vomiting, so use sparingly.
Season: Blooms May to July. Harvest roots in the fall after the first frost.

Habitat and range: Found in semidesert regions, canyon washes, prairies and roadsides in Utah, Colorado, Arizona, and New Mexico to the East Coast. Prefers dry, sandy soil and sunny locations.

Description: Perennial herb growing to 1 meter tall. Whorled leaves are alternate, lance-shaped, and 5–12 centimeters long. Inflorescence a cluster or umbel with up to 25 bright orange to yellow star-shaped flowers. Pollinated flowers turn to narrow light green seedpods up to 15 centimeters long. Mature seedpods open and release hundreds of flat, brown seeds.

Asclepias tuberosa growing in a cultivated garden
Jen Toews

Constituents: Cardiac glycosides, mucilaginous polysaccharides, tannins, alkaloids, bitter principles, quercetin, amino acids, resin

Medicinal actions: Diuretic, expectorant, diaphoretic, uterotonic

Cultivation: *A. tuberosa* prefers full sun and well-draining soil and is drought-tolerant once established. Milkweed attracts a variety of pollinating insects and is the host plant for monarch butterflies. Zones 3–9

The centuries old use of *Asclepias tuberosa* as an herbal remedy may have prompted the scientist Carl Linnaeus to name this species after the Greek god of medicine, Aesculapius. In the Rocky Mountains and Great Plains, this herb is important medicine for many Native American tribes. Cherokee use *A. tuberosa* as a potent herb for lung complaints, specifically for those involving coughing and increased mucus production. The root of milkweed opens airways, dilating the bronchioles, which makes breathing easier during respiratory illness. Historical documents and medical texts reveal this root, also called pleurisy root, was also used for more serious conditions including asthma, bronchitis, tuberculosis, and pleurisy.

Asclepias tuberosa in seed
Pat Horgan © Denver Botanic Gardens

Pleurisy root is a stimulating herb, especially for the vagus nerve which may lead to increased perspiration and dilation of the bronchioles. As a diaphoretic, pleurisy root helps the body cool down during feverish states. *A. tuberosa* also increases blood flow to the extremities, which may improve poor circulation that causes cold hands and feet. As a lymphagogue, take a small dose of pleurisy root tincture during illness for swollen lymph nodes and stagnation of the lymph system. This herb also stimulates digestion, due to its ability to increase the flow of digestive juices such as hydrochloric acid. The bitter principles within the root encourage food to move through, and out of the body, making it a great remedy for constipation. As a diuretic, pleurisy root stimulates the kidneys to increase urine output.

The rhizomes and roots of *Asclepias* should be dug from the ground in late fall after the first frost. In fact, this is true with all root medicine including echinacea, burdock, and pleurisy, as roots contain their highest concentration of medicine in the fall. Once a sizeable portion is dug up, thoroughly wash, cut up, and dry on a baking sheet. Fresh root can be tinctured as well, using 100 proof spirits.

Pleurisy Root Cold Infusion

Ingredients:

1 ounce dried pleurisy root
32 ounces water

Instructions:

Place the herb in a mason jar and add water. Cover the jar and let the mixture sit at room temperature overnight. Strain out root, and store in the refrigerator for up to 24 hours. Drink 2–4 ounces at a time, up to 3 times a day.

ASPARAGACEAE/ASPARAGUS FAMILY

Members of the asparagus family are monocots, usually having 3 sepals and 3 petals that are similar in size and color.

Yucca glauca growing near the Arikaree River in eastern Colorado
Jen Toews

YUCCA
Yucca spp.

Related species: *Y. baccata, Y. glauca, Y. harrimaniae*
Parts used: Flower, root, leaf
Cautions: Avoid prolonged ingestion of the root; avoid during pregnancy.
Season: Flowers May and June. Harvest root in the late fall after first frost.
Habitat and range: Dry, open sites, grasslands, and desert, throughout much of the western United States and southern Canada
Description: Evergreen perennial shrub to 3 meters tall, with erect stems and woody roots. Leaves are basal, to 91 centimeters long, stiff, and linear with sharp points. Flower stalks can reach 3 meters tall and contain bell-shaped flowers that range from creamy white to green. Fruits are hard pods or capsules with numerous black seeds.
Constituents: Proteins, carbohydrates, beta carotene, saponins, polyphenols
Medicinal actions: Anti-inflammatory, antiarthritic, nutritive, antioxidant

Cultivation: Yucca tolerates a variety of conditions but prefers full sun, and thrives in sandy, well-draining soil. Once established, yucca can tolerate periods of drought and low humidity. Zones 3–11 (varies by species).

Yucca is an extremely important ethnobotanical plant, providing food, medicine, tools, and many other functions for the Indigenous people and settlers of the southwestern United States. Nearly every part of the plant has been used for one purpose or another. One characteristic of yucca is the frayed fibers along the edges of the leaves. These fibers were stripped from the plant and woven into shoes, baskets, and rope. Ends of leaves were chewed or pounded to make paintbrushes, or the leaves' sharp ends could be transformed into a sewing needle.

Yucca glauca
Jen Toews

Yucca fruit is a staple for many Indigenous people of the Southwest including the Navajo, Arapaho, and Cherokee. Fruits can be eaten raw or roasted like potatoes, or dried and stored for the winter. Spring flowers are collected and added to soups or even eaten raw.

The root of *Yucca* contains saponins and resveratrol which have been studied for their effects on arthritic pain. A weak decoction of yucca root, about 8 grams of peeled root placed in 16 ounces of boiling water and steeped for 10 minutes, can be sipped throughout the day for relief from joint inflammation, swelling, and pain. This weak decoction has also shown promise in lowering blood cholesterol and triglycerides and improving gut flora. Grated root can be applied directly to the skin to reduce inflammation and stop bleeding. Juiced root can also relieve rash from poison ivy. The saponins in yucca root can be extracted and used for an effective soap or shampoo. This solution acts as a surfactant, helping to

Yucca glauca in habitat
Jen Toews

wash bacteria and dirt away from surfaces. Yucca soap solution was once a common remedy for head lice.

Yucca Root Shampoo

This recipe requires a food processor or blender, funnel, and fine mesh strainer. While working with raw yucca root, it is important to wash your hands while handling. If using dried yucca root, rehydrate in water for 12 hours before attempting this recipe. This soap can be used just like shampoo or body wash.

Ingredients:

½ cup fresh yucca root, chopped into 1-inch pieces
4 cups distilled water

Instructions:

Place chopped yucca root in a blender and add distilled water. Blend thoroughly for at least 2 minutes, then strain to remove the liquid and separate the solids. Use a funnel to pour the liquid soap into a clean glass jar. Store in the refrigerator for 1 week or freeze until needed.

ASTERACEAE/ASTER FAMILY

Annual, biennial, and perennial herbaceous plants with dense flowerheads surrounded by involucral bracts

Arnica fulgens, foothill arnica, can be found dotting prairies and grasslands as well as montane forests in western North America.
Mike Kintgen

ACHILLEA MILLEFOLIUM
Yarrow

Achillea millefolium is a popular plant for native and pollinator-themed gardens.
Jen Toews

Composite flowers of *Achillea millefolium*
Jen Toews

Also called: Carpenter's weed, herba militaris, milfoil, nosebleed, soldier's woundwort

Parts used: Flower and leaf

Cautions: Use in moderation during pregnancy.

Season: Blooms June to October. Harvest flowers at the height of bloom. Leaves can be harvested spring until fall.

Habitat and range: Yarrow grows in many ecosystems including sunny grasslands, pastures, disturbed soils, near roadsides, and high alpine environments. Yarrow is found throughout the Northern Hemisphere, including the Rocky Mountains, at elevations ranging from sea level to 11,500 feet.

Description: Yarrow is an herbaceous, rhizomatous perennial growing to 1 meter tall. The soft, downy leaves (3–10 centimeters long) are bipinnate or tripinnate and grow in whorls along the stem. The flower head is a flat-topped cluster of numerous ray and disc flowers, which are subtended by bracts. White ray flowers are oval or round and surround yellow disc flowers. Yarrow has a complex smell, a mix of peppery spice and floral notes.

Constituents: Volatile oils (including borneol, camphor, linalool, pinene, azulene), sesquiterpene lactones, flavonoids, alkaloids, tannins, triterpenes

Medicinal actions: Antispasmodic, digestive, diaphoretic, anti-inflammatory, astringent, antimicrobial, styptic, emmenagogue, mild diuretic

Cultivation: Plant yarrow in a sunny location in well-draining soil. Deadheading yarrow may encourage a second round of blooms. Provide supplemental water during times of drought. Zones 3–9

Yarrow contains a complex mixture of phytochemicals which contribute to its wide-ranging healing abilities. The healing properties of the yarrow flower have been utilized by many civilizations across the globe for thousands of years. In fact, recent evidence suggests that Neanderthals may have used yarrow 50,000 years ago as an herbal remedy. *Achillea millefolium* translates to "Achilles's thousand-leaved herb." Folk legends state that the Trojan War hero Achilles and his soldiers used yarrow to treat wounds on the battlefield.

Yarrow has an affinity for working on the circulatory system, helping to tone veins, capillaries, and arteries. Yarrow may help regulate blood pressure, reduce menstrual bleeding, and has become a trusted herb to stop nosebleeds, quell hemorrhaging, and subdue bleeding wounds. Yarrow tea is a great remedy for colds and flu. Due to its diaphoretic properties, yarrow can help to reduce a fever during illness. High levels of flavonoids in the yarrow seem to cause the blood to thin slightly, and relax the capillaries within the body, causing a drop in internal temperature.

Due to the antibacterial and healing properties of yarrow, minor cuts and wounds may benefit greatly from a yarrow wash. These properties also make yarrow a trusted ally for oral health. A yarrow decoction, or tincture diluted with water, effectively cleanses the mouth of bacterial buildup when gargled. Finally, the astringent properties may ease minor bleeding of the gums and tighten and tone the gum tissues.

Yarrow also serves as a natural bug repellent. Many Native American tribes use yarrow for repellent and hang bundles of yarrow outside of dwellings and spray yarrow tea on fish and meat to repel flies and other insects. Farmers place a sprig of fresh yarrow in their ears to repel insects around their face. Some birds including common starling use yarrow in their nests, which inhibits parasitic growth and wards off insects.

Yarrow Wound Powder

Ingredients:

Dried flowers and leaves of yarrow plant

Instructions:

Using the dried flowers and leaves of yarrow, process the herb into a fine powder using a spice or coffee grinder. Store powder in a sterile jar or container. For topical use, sprinkle yarrow powder directly on minor wounds. The powder can also be added to hot water for tea and washes or made into a healing salve.

Cold and Flu Tea

Ingredients:

1 cup dried yarrow flower
1 cup dried elder flower
1 cup dried peppermint leaves
Boiling water

Instructions:

Measure equal parts dried yarrow flower, dried elder flower, and dried peppermint leaves. Blend these plants in a container until well mixed. To prepare a tea, measure 1 tablespoon of the blend, place in a cup, and add boiling water. Cover the container and allow to steep for at least 5 minutes. Strain and drink warm.

PEARLY EVERLASTING
Anaphalis margaritacea

Also called: Western pearly everlasting

Parts used: Leaf and flower

Season: July to October. Harvest leaves in the spring and early summer. Harvest flowers at the height of their bloom.

Habitat and range: Pearly everlasting grows in meadows, hillsides, and open forests from foothills to subalpine zones of the Rocky Mountains and throughout the United States. Native to North America and Asia, this species has naturalized in some areas of Europe.

Anaphalis margaritacea
Jen Toews

Description: This showy, rhizomatous, colony-forming, perennial herb grows from 20–60 centimeters tall. Stems sturdy and erect. Leaves alternate along stem, often at a 45-degree angle, lance-shaped, 3–10 centimeters long, and woolly. Numerous flowers to 10 millimeters across in dense corymbs, which resemble pearls. Thin, papery, white bracts surround yellowish-brown disc florets.

Constituents: Flavonoids, diterpenes, hydroxylactones

Medicinal actions: Antibacterial, analgesic, astringent, expectorant, sedative

Cultivation: Plant *Anaphalis margaritacea* in full sun or partial shade in well-draining soil. Sow seeds in the fall or spring, sprinkling them on the soil surface and keeping them uncovered. Zones 3–7

Thin, papery bracts surround the disc flowers.
Jen Toews

Most of the ethnobotanical knowledge we have about pearly everlasting involves Indigenous people's uses of the plant. For centuries, people have burned plants including *Anaphalis* for various reasons. Smoke from plants flavors meats, preserves fish, and keeps pests and bugs away. Inhaling smoke in small quantities can improve lung ailments, including asthma and bronchitis, and may relieve pain and encourage healing after injury. Furthermore, burning plants is a spiritual practice, believed to cleanse the mind, body, and homes and dwellings. The Cheyenne fumigate homes with pearly everlasting to keep negative energy away. During a prayer ceremony, Native Americans burn *Anaphalis* as songs are sung and prayers are spoken—the smoke carries these words up to the heavens where the gods reside.

While this plant contains important medicinal properties on par with *Arnica* and yarrow, it is often overlooked in modern herbalism. As an astringent with antibacterial properties, pearly everlasting has useful applications as a skin ally. Bruises, minor swelling, and burns would benefit from a tincture, poultice, strong tea, salve, or bath of pearly everlasting. *Anaphalis margaritacea* also shows antiasthmatic, anti-coughing, expectorant, and anti-inflammatory activity, according to the *World Journal of Pharmaceutical Research*. Thus, consider using *Anaphalis* in a cough syrup or tea blend as a natural expectorant and to support the lungs.

Pearly Everlasting Smoke Bundles

Smoke bundles made of pearly everlasting can be used for minor lung complaints or ceremonially in any indoor or outdoor space.

Materials needed:

Fresh *Anaphalis*, stems and flowers
String

Instructions:

Harvest 2 small bouquets (10 stems per bouquet) of fresh *Anaphalis* flowers and stems. Dry plant material for 2 to 3 days on a baking sheet or wire rack, ensuring plant material is separated to prevent mold. Gather 10 stems of pearly everlasting and carefully form into a bundle. Using very thin string, tie and knot around the base of the bundle. Wind string around the plant material to keep the bundle together, then tie and knot at the other end. Store in a cool, dry place. To burn, light one end of the bundle until a flame forms, then blow out flame. As smoke forms, slowly wave the bundle around a room or waft slowly on and around the body.

BURDOCK
Arctium lappa

Also called: Bardane (French), beggar's buttons, fox's clout, Gobo (Japanese), great burdock, thorny burr

Parts used: Root, leaf, seed

Cautions: None known

Season: Blooms August to October. Harvest root in the fall after the first frost.

Habitat and range: *Arctium lappa* is a European native that has established itself around the world. Great burdock grows sporadically throughout the Rocky Mountains, from Colorado to Montana, the Great Plains, and Northeast in moist fertile soils and riparian areas.

Description: Burdock is a hefty biennial herb with a spacious presence both in the wild and home garden. It can reach heights of 2 meters and a spread of over 1 meter, especially in nitrogen rich soils, but size can vary greatly. During its first year, a large rosette

Thistle-like flowers of *Arctium lappa*
Mike Kintgen

forms, with cordate leaves to 50 centimeters long and 30 centimeters wide. The leaves are broad near the base, becoming narrow at the tip. Leaves are coarse above and finely woolly below. During the spring and summer of the plant's second year, the stem rises from the root reaching 1.2 meters and branching at the top. Late summer flowers are pink to purple, very round and thistlelike. Several rows of hooked bracts are present at the base of each flower. Flower heads are 1 to 3 centimeters across. After the flowers fade, the bristles stiffen into a burr which encases numerous shiny seeds. The sturdy taproot is dark brown on the outside and white or tan on the inside.

Constituents: Inulin, mucilage, chlorogenic acid, complex sugars, bitter compounds, glucoside, tannic acid; root may contain up to 40 percent of the polysaccharide inulin.

Medicinal actions: Alterative, diuretic, diaphoretic, nutritive, emollient, and demulcent

First-year rosette with large leaves
Jen Toews

Cultivation: Burdock seeds can be directly sown into the soil after danger of last frost. Germination takes 1–2 weeks. Burdock is a biennial, prefers full sun to partial shade, and well-draining soil. Root can be harvested after 90 days. Zones 2–10

The name *Arctium lappa* is derived from the Greek word for bear, *arktos*, and *lappa* means "to seize." One of burdock's renowned characteristics is the burrs that attach so efficiently to clothing and fur. In fact, the Swiss inventor George de Mestral was so fascinated by burdock seeds and their hooking mechanism that he studied the anatomy of the dried burdock flowerheads, which led to the creation of Velcro Companies.

Ancient texts and historical records spanning the globe have documented the many medicinal uses of burdock root, leaf, and seed. Native American tribes, medieval herbalists of Europe, and healers in India and China all have relied upon the healing qualities of burdock. Native Americans use infusions of the root, leaves, and seeds for kidney stones, scurvy, and arthritic complaints. Hildegard of Bingen, a medieval German herbalist, documented several success stories using burdock root to treat cancerous tumors. In East Asia, burdock became well respected as a cell regenerator and detoxifier, especially helpful with urinary issues and chronic skin conditions.

Many medicinal texts have labeled burdock as a "blood purifier," meaning that the root contains powerful constituents to cleanse blood. Although burdock root does not directly purify the blood, it does contain compounds that support the organs of the body that metabolize and cleanse. The more precise term to describe this medical action is *alterative*, meaning it makes the systems of the body work more efficiently.

Consider burdock a deep-seated medicine, requiring patience and time. Burdock uses its cooling, calming, and nourishing energy to heal the body slowly and deeply. Herbalist Matthew Wood states: "Burdock increases bile secretion to digest oily foods better, increases oil uptake and liver processing of lipids, and distributes lipids to the skin, hair, tissues, adrenals, steroids and hormonal system." In addition, burdock root, leaf, and seeds work to improve digestion, ease inflammation of the skin, and promote balance throughout the body.

The complex sugars, bitter components, mucilage, and pectin found in burdock root work primarily on the digestive system. Burdock root may contain up to 40 percent inulin, which is an oligosaccharide (also found in the roots of dandelion, chicory, and Jerusalem artichoke). Inulin is an indigestible sugar which has been shown to moderate blood sugar and promote gut health as a prebiotic. Burdock stimulates digestive juice secretion for efficient digestion and nutrient absorption and supports kidney and liver function. When our digestive system is working efficiently and properly, our skin clears, our mood improves, and our vitality strengthens.

As a skin ally, Burdock works slowly but effectively to treat conditions such as acne, psoriasis, dandruff, and eczema. For chronic skin conditions, it's best to drink an infusion of burdock root regularly for an extended period. Burdock leaves contain a mucilage component which acts as a demulcent and emollient. Mash up burdock leaves to create a poultice to relieve bruises, skin inflammation, and swellings.

In addition to an infusion and poultice, another excellent way to preserve fresh burdock is to tincture it. Tincturing in 50 percent alcohol preserves important constituents from the root such as the prebiotic inulin, and caffeoylquinic acid, a beneficial antioxidant found in the root. Mashed seeds can also be tinctured. Harvest burdock root in the fall of its first year or in the spring of its second year of growth. Harvesting at this time will ensure high amounts of inulin and other beneficial compounds. Leaves can be harvested at any time, but preferably in midsummer when they are most robust. Seeds are collected when ripe. Shake or crush the spent flowerheads to release the seeds, then dry in the shade.

Burdock Pickles

Burdock root is a popular vegetable in Japan, as well as in other parts of Asia and Europe. Many of the medicinal benefits of burdock can be easily assimilated in the body by simply eating it raw or in dishes such as stir-frys and soup. The texture is crunchy like a carrot and the taste is earthy and sweet.

Ingredients:

2 to 3 medium-sized burdock roots (cleaned)
3 garlic cloves, sliced
4 ginger slices
16-ounce bottle of apple cider vinegar
16-ounce bottle of fermented soy sauce

Instructions:

Cut the roots into 1- to 2-inch-long segments, and then thinly slice or julienne them. Place prepared burdock into a pan and just cover with water. Bring the water to a boil for 2–3 minutes to soften the roots, then remove from heat. Remove the roots using a slotted spoon and place them in a clean bowl, reserving the cooking liquid. Add thin slices of ginger and garlic to the burdock and stir. Divide this mixture into 2 or 3 sterilized mason jars, filling them to about 1 inch from the top. In each jar, fill ¼ of the volume with apple cider vinegar, ¼ with fermented soy sauce, and ½ with the burdock cooking liquid. Cap tightly. Refrigerate until ready to use, or place in a pressure cooker or water bath to seal and make shelf stable.

ARNICA
Arnica cordifolia

Also called: Heartleaf arnica, leopard's bane
Related species: *A. chamissonis, A. latifolia, A. mollis*
Parts used: Leaf and flower
Cautions: Arnica is for external use only. Ingesting or applying arnica to broken skin is not recommended.
Season: Blooms June to August. Harvest flowers at peak bloom.
Habitat and range: *Arnica cordifolia* is found in open woods and shady areas from submontane to subalpine throughout the Rocky Mountains and western United States and Canada.
Description: *Arnica* are perennial herbs, which grow to 60 centimeters tall and spread vigorously through slender rhizomes. Leaves are opposite, attached to a long petiole, and have toothed margins and downy surfaces. Lower leaves are cordate and up to 10 centimeters long, while upper leaves are much smaller. Daisy-like flowers are yellow, 2–6 centimeters wide, with up to

A colony of *Arnica cordifolia* growing in a montane forest
Jen Toews © Denver Botanic Gardens

16 rays surrounding golden disc florets. After the bloom fades, a hairy achene with a tuft of white, barbed bristles persists.
Constituents: Sesquiterpenoid lactones, flavonoids, coumarins, volatile oil, polysaccharides, phenolic acids, polyacetylenes, carotenoids
Medicinal actions: Anti-inflammatory, rubefacient, analgesic, antibacterial, antifungal
Cultivation: *A. chamissonis* and *A. latifolia* grow well in a garden setting. Arnica prefers moist, well-draining soil with a pH between 6.0 and 8.0. Fertilize in the spring with a layer of organic compost or fertilizer. Arnica blooms best in full sun, but protect from drought and intense heat by planting in an area with some afternoon shade. Zones 1–9

Arnica has a reputation around the world as a powerful herbal medicine for injuries of the muscular and skeletal systems. Germans commonly refer to arnica as *wundkraut,* "wound herb," and *fallkraut,* "fall herb." The phrase "*stoh up un goh hen,*" which translates to "stand up and go home," has been used to describe arnica and attests to its fast-healing properties. German-led Commission E, an advisory board of doctors, healers, and scientists which studies the efficacy of herbs, concludes that arnica is suitable treatment for

Arnica parryi almost always lacks ray flowers when blooming.
Mike Kintgen

inflammation, bruising pain, and swelling caused by injury, rheumatism, or insect bites.

Arnica's pain-relieving properties, and its ability to heal physical injuries such as bruises and sprains, make this herb an important remedy worth keeping on hand. A liniment of arnica is great for joint inflammation, sore muscles, and back pain. Oils fortified with arnica can be easily applied as a compress on bruises. And with the addition of beeswax, oils can be transformed into salves and ointments for a more stable and creamier product. In homeopathic medicine, arnica is specifically recommended for traumatic injuries and experiences where the subject feels "knocked out of the body" or is in a state of psychological shock, for example, after a car accident or surgical procedure. In this case, arnica medicine is administered in homeopathic pills in which the constituents are extremely diluted and safe to consume.

Consider bringing medicine-making supplies on a hike to instantly submerge the arnica as the arnica flowers quickly break down after harvest. Plant oils (olive oil or coconut oil) or alcohol are the best vehicle for extracting the beneficial sesquiterpenoid lactones in the flower head. When arnica is placed in an alcohol such as vodka or rubbing alcohol, the medicine is concentrated and easy to apply. If harvesting is sparse, arnica is readily available in stores and pharmacies in the form of gels, ointments, and creams.

Arnica Liniment

Arnica liniment is suitable for minor bumps, bruises, and sprains. Use fresh arnica whenever possible.

Ingredients:

4–5 cups fresh arnica flowers
16 ounces rubbing alcohol

Instructions:

Fill mason jar or lidded container of your choice ¾ full of fresh arnica flowers. Pour rubbing alcohol over flowers, then seal jar and label. Shake the jar daily to agitate the mixture. After 3 weeks, strain and bottle.

To use arnica liniment, soak a paper towel or washcloth in hot water and then pour arnica liniment on the towel. Tightly wrap the towel or cloth around the injured area for 15 minutes. Repeat as needed.

BIG SAGEBRUSH
Artemisia tridentata

Also called: Basin sagebrush, blue sagebrush, Great Basin sagebrush
Related species: *A. frigida, A. ludoviciana*
Parts used: Leaf and flower
Cautions: Extremely bitter; avoid during pregnancy
Season: Blooms July to October. Harvest leaves year-round, and flowers at the height of their bloom.
Habitat and range: Grows in valleys, parks, and on slopes, from the plains to montane; found throughout the Rocky Mountain region and western North America

Artemisia tridentata
Cindy Newlander © Denver Botanic Gardens

Description: *Artemisia tridentata* is a multibranched shrub with silvery-blue or green fragrant foliage that grows from 0.5 to 3 meters tall. The root system contains a long taproot to 4 meters, as well as secondary roots which spread just below the soil. Stems are gray, and younger stems are hairy, while older stems are hairless and covered in a thin papery bark. Leaves, 1–3 centimeters long, are alternate, wedge-shaped, 3-toothed at tips, and covered with feltlike hairs. Yellow flowers on spikes (panicles) are small with hairy bracts and sometimes surrounded with small leaves.
Constituents: Camphor, essential oils, pinene, beta thujone, cineole, sesquiterpenoids
Medicinal actions: Antirheumatic, digestive, disinfectant, sedative, febrifuge
Cultivation: Sagebrush thrives in gardens where moisture and nutrients are scarce. Plant in well-draining soil with a bit of sand or rocks to prevent standing water. Sagebrush is perfect for xeric gardens that are exposed to full sun and wind. Once established, no supplemental water is necessary. Zones 4–10

Artemisia frigida, prairie sagewort, spreads by underground rhizomes.
Jen Toews

Artemisia tridentata is the iconic shrub of the American West. One of the most abundant shrubs in North America, it covers millions of acres of land from Colorado to California, and from New Mexico to Montana. This species is important to Indigenous populations of the American West who have used it reliably as a digestive aid, cold and cough remedy, antidiarrheal, eyewash, diaphoretic, emetic, and as an antidote for poisoning.

Artemisia is as useful today as it has been for centuries. In fact, herbalist Michael Moore compares sagebrush leaves to clay: They are elegant and useful with the ability to be molded into almost any remedy. A sagebrush tea contains bitter principles, which promote digestion and elimination. A hot tea induces sweating, which cools the body during a feverish state. And due to its antibacterial properties *Artemisia* holds some promise in treating infections of the skin, gums, and mucosal membranes. One note of caution: Sagebrush tea is extremely bitter and unpalatable for many. Thus the cold infusion method is preferred which results in a much smoother flavor. To make a cold infusion, pack the plant material in a tea bag and place the bag in a jar of cold water to steep for 24 hours.

Another way to obtain the benefits of *Artemisia*'s healing essential oils is to breathe in the vapors or smoke. Inhaling sagebrush steam can help the lungs expel mucus and quicken recovery from a cough. This method is especially reliable during cold and flu season, or to treat bronchitis. The same is true with the smoke of *Artemisia*, which contains essential oils that can be healing for the lungs and also cleanse the surrounding air. A 2007 study of medicinal smoke

Artemisia ludoviciana, white sagebrush, is mostly found west of the Mississippi River.
Jen Toews

concludes that the use of herbs like *A. tridentata* can reduce airborne pathogenic bacteria within a confined space (Nautiyal, Chauhan, and Nene, 2007). To smudge with sagebrush, harvest a bundle, then dry it to use later as a smoke for the home. Smudging with herbs is useful in removing unwanted odors, uplifting the mood of a space, and even removing toxins and bacteria lingering in the air.

Sagebrush Steam Inhalation

Try this steam inhalation as an alternative to drinking sagebrush tea. The antibacterial vapors of *Artemisia* act as an expectorant, helping lungs release unwanted mucus while fighting infection.

Materials Needed:

2–3 quarts water
2 large bundles of sagebrush (fresh or dried)
Large mixing bowl
Bath towel

Instructions:

Bring 2–3 quarts of water to a boil in a tea kettle. Place the bundles of sagebrush in a large mixing bowl, then pour the boiling water over the herbs. Immediately place your head over the bowl, covering it with a large towel to prevent the vapors from escaping. Slowly inhale the vapors. Repeat with another round of boiling water.

ARROWLEAF BALSAMROOT
Balsamorhiza sagittata

Also called: Balsamroot, *Wyethia sagittata*
Related species: *B. incana, B. macrophylla, Wyethia amplexicaulis*
Parts used: Root
Cautions: Avoid during pregnancy.
Season: Blooms April to July. Harvest the root in the fall after the first frost.
Habitat and range: Dry hillsides, woods, or open meadows from foothills to montane; Rocky Mountains and western North America from North Dakota to Arizona and California
Description: Perennial herb from 20 to 70 centimeters tall with aromatic taproot and hairy leaves. Basal leaves are arrow-shaped, up to 30 centimeters long and 15 centimeters wide; stem leaves are small and alternate. Yellow flowers are 6 to 11 centimeters across, with bright yellow ray florets and dark yellow disc florets.
Constituents: Flavonoids, resin, triterpenoids, aromatic oils, inulin

Balsamorhiza sagittata has arrowhead-shaped leaves.
Mike Kintgen © Denver Botanic Gardens

Medicinal actions: Expectorant, diaphoretic, antifungal, antimicrobial, rubefacient
Cultivation: Balsamroot prefers full sun, sandy or loamy soils. Because this plant does not transplant well, it is best to grow from seed. Zones 4–8

The medicine of arrowleaf balsamroot works well for a broad range of respiratory complaints that affect the lungs, throat, and nasal passages. Its antimicrobial and expectorant properties work to heal the body and lungs from several angles. Balsamroot contains immune-stimulating and antiviral properties, much like its close cousin *Echinacea*. Research on *Echinacea* shows its ability to increase the amount of disease-fighting white blood cells. That said, balsamroot is most effective during the early stages of an impending common cold or flu, attacking the infection before it settles in.

Balsamroot is also used by herbalists to treat both acute and chronic cough. The constituents of balsamroot help loosen stubborn mucus that irritates the lungs, thus increasing the productivity of a cough. Drink several cups of very warm balsamroot decoction throughout the day to ease symptoms. A syrup made with honey and balsamroot works particularly well, since honey alone is a soothing remedy for coughs. For a sore throat, add 20 drops of balsamroot tincture to a teaspoon of honey and swallow.

Balsamroot has also shown promise as a disinfectant and rubefacient. Its antimicrobial properties help soothe urethritis and complications due to a UTI. The Cheyenne find *B. sagitatta* to be helpful as a diuretic and to treat inflammation and pain of the urinary tract. The Blackfoot and Shoshoni tribes utilize its antimicrobial properties to treat skin sores, wounds, and inflamed skin. When applied topically, balsamroot opens capillaries and blood vessels, which, in turn, increases blood

Balsamorhiza sagittata growing on a dry hillside
Mike Kintgen

flow and oxygenation. These rubefacient properties make it an effective treatment for muscle aches and joint pain. Steep balsamroot in a carrier oil such as olive or grapeseed oil for 2 weeks, strain, and rub oil on affected areas.

Balsamroot Cough Syrup

Because honey has some medicinal properties, this cough syrup contains raw honey rather than white sugar. If a less sweet syrup is preferred, use less honey. The addition of alcohol preserves the syrup and prevents mold from forming.

Ingredients:

16 ounces water
1 cup finely chopped balsamroot
8 ounces raw honey
1 ounce 80 proof liquor

Instructions:

Pour water into a saucepan, add chopped root, and bring to a boil, uncovered. Reduce to a simmer and cook until approximately 8 ounces of liquid remain. Turn off heat and strain liquid into a mason jar. Add honey and liquor and stir. Label and refrigerate up to several weeks or freeze.

CHICORY
Cichorium intybus

Also called: Blue sailors, coffeeweed, succory

Parts used: Root, leaf, flower

Cautions: None known

Season: Blooms July to October. Harvest the root in the fall after the first frost.

Habitat and range: Found in lower elevation fields, open meadows, and disturbed areas throughout the United States

Description: Chicory is a tall and scraggly perennial herb growing to 180 centimeters. At the plant's base, the rosette leaves, which are lancelike, deeply lobed, and hairy, resemble dandelion leaves. As the leaves travel up the stem, they become smaller, less lobed, and widely spaced. Breaking off a small portion of the stem will produce a milky white sap. Flowers are 2–4 centimeters wide, sky blue or light purple, and sometimes white or pink. Flower heads contain 2 rows of involucral bracts: The inner bracts are longer and erect, while the outer bracts are shorter and spreading. The ends of the petals are usually toothed.

Constituents: Inulin, quercetin, bitter principles, phenolic acids, flavonoids

Medicinal actions: Bitter tonic, laxative, nutritive, diuretic

Cichorium intybus growing along a gravel road, a common place to spot this species
Jen Toews

Cichorium intybus
Jen Toews © Denver Botanic Gardens

Cultivation: Chicory thrives in full sun, moist soil, and a garden free of weeds and high in organic matter. Sow seed in spring, as early as 2 to 3 weeks before the average last frost date. Please note that this species is on the Colorado Noxious Weed List and therefore is not legal to cultivate in Colorado. Be mindful of this species' growth and spread elsewhere if cultivating or consider buying plant parts needed for medicinal preparations from a reputable source instead of growing. Zones 3–10

Once considered a worthless roadside weed, chicory's young leaves are prized by chefs and foodies alike for their robust and pungent flavor. Flowers and leaves, although quite bitter, can be added to salads and sautés. Harvest young tender leaves in the spring for a less bitter taste. The roots are also edible but very bitter and may require several changes of water before eating.

The bitter components of the leaf, flower, and root are arguably the most important qualities of this plant. Although bitterness is a taste profile that some humans consider off-putting as the American diet leans strongly toward sweet and salty, rather than bitter, it is important to include bitter flavors in our diet. This is because digestion begins in the mouth: When something bitter is tasted, the salivary glands are activated and digestion begins. Bitter plants like chicory improve the digestive process overall as they also tonify the digestive organs and increase assimilation of nutrients.

Another important component of chicory is inulin, a polysaccharide acting as dietary fiber, which is also beneficial to the digestive system. Found in the roots of chicory, dandelion, and burdock, inulin is considered a prebiotic and is indigestible by humans. While the molecules of inulin cannot break down in the small intestine, they travel to the lower gut and feed the beneficial bacteria of the digestive system. It is common to see inulin added to cereal bars, dairy products, and baked goods as a sugar or fat replacement, and to improve the overall health benefits of a food product. Decocting or tincturing the root will draw out the inulin efficiently. This tincture can be taken daily as a prebiotic or when experiencing minor indigestion or stomach complaints.

Perhaps the most well-known use of chicory root is as a coffee substitute. This was first documented in 18th-century Europe when coffee was banned by Frederick the Great. He viewed beer as a more wholesome and nutritious beverage than coffee. During this time, an innkeeper from Brunswick discovered that roasted chicory root had a similar flavor profile to the roasted coffee bean. Its popularity as a coffee alternative spread across Europe. Chicory root was also used as a coffee substitute in the United States during the Civil War, when Union naval blockades prevented coffee from entering Louisiana's ports. Finally, because it is much cheaper than coffee, it was also used in prisons.

Chicory root coffee is high in chlorogenic acid and other compounds which have been shown to improve gut health, regulate blood sugar, and may have anticancer properties. Roots are dried, roasted, and ground up and the resulting taste is earthy, slightly bitter, and nutty, similar to coffee.

Chicory Coffee

The coffee-like beverage contains no caffeine, yet has the earthiness and bitterness of coffee beans. Modify this recipe by adding equal parts ground coffee for added caffeine and flavor.

Ingredients:

3 tablespoons chicory root
1 tablespoon burdock root
¼ teaspoon cinnamon
8–12 ounces boiling water

Instructions:

Place ingredients into a jar. Pour 8–12 ounces of boiling water (depending on strength desired) over the roots and cover. Allow to steep for a minimum of 5 minutes. Strain and enjoy.

CURLYCUP GUMWEED
Grindelia squarrosa

Resinous sap is found on *Grindelia squarrosa.*
Jen Toews © Denver Botanic Gardens

Grindelia squarrosa in full bloom
Mike Kintgen

Also called: Grindelia, gumweed, rosinweed

Related species: *G. hirsutula, G. subalpina*

Parts used: Leaf, flower

Cautions: Avoid ingesting this herb for extended periods of time or in large quantities.

Season: Blooms July to September. Harvest flowers at the peak of their bloom when sap is present.

Habitat and range: Prefers sandy and clay soils in dry, arid spaces in the foothills of the Rocky Mountains, and throughout much of the United States

Description: *Grindelia squarrosa* is an annual, biennial, or perennial many-branched herb that grows to 1 meter tall or is decumbent (lying on the ground). The leaves are 2–7 centimeters, hairless, and with round-toothed margins. The terminal flowers are 2–3 centimeters across with numerous disc and ray florets; rays are sometimes absent. Young flower buds are very sticky and covered in a thick white sap. Bracts or phyllaries arch and curve backwards.

Constituents: Diterpenes (grindelic acid), essential oils, tannins, flavonoids (including quercetin), resins

Medicinal actions: Expectorant, antispasmodic, sedative, hypotensive, rubefacient

Cultivation: Direct sow this perennial in the fall or spring, or propagate in containers and transplant. Grindelia prefers full sun and well-drained soil. Once established, grindelia requires little care and tolerates dry conditions. Zones 4–8

Grindelia is a genus of plants that has been used as medicine by Native American tribes for centuries. The Costanoan Indians boil leaves and flowerheads of gumweed for healing dermatitis caused by poison oak, and for wounds, burns, boils, and sores (Bocek, 1984; Foster, 2002). The Kawaiisu people discovered the flower and leaf contained analgesic properties which they used to treat sore muscles. These Native American remedies are so effective that many were adopted by early physicians of frontier medicine and are still used today.

Herbalists today respect grindelia for its broad spectrum of healing benefits. A tea or tincture of grindelia flowers and leaves is a trustworthy remedy for respiratory complaints including dry lungs and to help loosen phlegm. In addition, grindelia relaxes both smooth muscle and cardiac muscles, which makes it effective in treating asthmatic and bronchial issues associated with increased heart rate, rapid pulse, or any raced response of the nervous system. Finally, grindelia's relaxant and sedative properties calm breathing and may reduce blood pressure. Consider adding *Grindelia* to a nighttime cough formula to promote sleep.

Grindelia leaf and flower stimulate skin cell regeneration, reduce inflammation, increase blood flow to the surface of the skin, and even possess antimicrobial properties. Thus, there is potential for grindelia to be used to treat skin ailments such as insect bites, irritation, and burns. Make a poultice or a strong tea from the aerial parts and apply to the affected areas. Or dilute a grindelia tincture with warm water and apply. For a topical wash to keep at home or in a first aid kit, add fresh or dried *Grindelia* to witch hazel and let steep for a week. Since *Grindelia* is a selenium accumulator, high concentrations of this element are often present in the plant. Grindelia should be used with caution: as a low dose herb, a little goes a long way. Additionally, when not used judiciously, the resin in the flower heads can negatively impact the kidneys. One cup of grindelia flower tea or a few drops of tincture in a glass of water is a great place to start.

Grindelia Tincture

Harvest grindelia when in full bloom and when sap is present and only harvest the top ⅔ of the plant.

Ingredients:

1 cup grindelia flower tops
16 ounces 100 proof vodka or spirits

Instructions:

Place grindelia flowers in a 1-pint mason jar. Pour 100 proof vodka over the herb until the flowers are completely submerged in alcohol. Seal the jar and shake vigorously. Label the mixture and store in a cool, dark place. Shake daily to encourage maceration. After 3 to 4 weeks, strain the tincture into a new jar. Seal the jar and label.

PRICKLY LETTUCE
Lactuca serriola

Also called: Compass plant, scarole, wild lettuce
Related species: *L. canadensis, L. tatarica*
Parts used: Leaf, seed
Cautions: Consuming large amounts of the leaves can be toxic. Avoid during pregnancy and lactation.
Season: Blooms May to August. Leaves can be harvested from spring until frost.
Habitat and range: Found in man-made or naturally disturbed sites, meadows, and open spaces from plains to montane; widespread throughout the United States
Description: Annual with strong central stem, unbranching until flowering stems are present, growing to 2 meters tall. Leaves are alternate, lance-shaped, with lobes that usually point back toward the stem (like dandelion). Leaves with prickles along the margins and underside of central vein. Leaves and stems exude a milky sap when torn or cut. Flowers to 13 millimeters wide, pale yellow, and with 15–20 ray flowers.

Lactuca serriola
Jen Toews

Constituents: Bitter principles (lactucin, lactucopicrin, lactucic acid), triterpenes, phytosterols, plant organic acids
Medicinal actions: Sedative, hypnotic, analgesic, antispasmodic
Cultivation: This annual grows easily in full sun, prefers well-draining, sandy soils. Self-sowing. Zones 5–9

The milky white sap, or latex, found in *Lactuca serriola* holds the medicine of this plant. It contains lactucarium and other sesquiterpenoid lactones, which have a sedative and analgesic effect on the body. Historical records indicate Ancient Egyptians used *Lactuca* spp. for pain relief, and during the late 18th century, *L. serriola* was sold as a drug in the United States, sometimes under the name "Lettuce Opium." A recent study by the *Journal of Ethnopharmacology* concluded

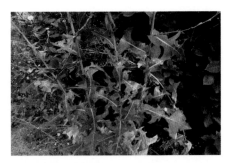
Leaves' lobes point back toward stem
Jen Toews

the analgesic compounds found in *L. serriola* are similar to ibuprofen (Wesolowska et al., 2006). Sciatica, migraines, and sore joints and muscles are just a few examples of conditions that can be treated by this analgesic herb.

Prickly lettuce is an effective pain reliever on its own, or in conjunction with other herbs. Cannabis, California poppy, and peppermint are some pain-relieving herbs that are compatible with prickly lettuce. When pain is accompanied with inflammation, combine prickly lettuce with anti-inflammatory herbs such as ginger, turmeric, or chamomile. As this plant also works on the nervous system to calm and relax, those suffering from insomnia, hyperactivity, or stress could benefit from a tincture or tea of wild lettuce.

To capture the highest amount of pain-relieving and sedative compounds from the latex, harvest this plant at first flower. Remove the flower heads of the plant and scrape the oozing sap into a vessel, continuing this process until the plant is exhausted of the latex. Allow the sap to dry before using. A tincture of the fresh plant is another way to make an effective, less labor-intensive remedy.

Wild Lettuce Tincture

Try wild lettuce tincture to relieve minor pains or help with insomnia. This tincture can be taken straight, or added to a nighttime tea, or even a glass of water.

Ingredients:

4 cups fresh wild lettuce, chopped
4 cups 100 proof vodka

Instructions:

Cut the wild lettuce plant at the base. Chop the leaves and upper stems into 1- to 2-inch pieces, and let the cuttings fall directly into a 1-quart mason jar to preserve the sap. Fill the jar with cuttings, lightly packing down to fit more plant material. When the jar is ¾ full, add 100 proof vodka, ensuring the cuttings are submerged. Seal the jar and label. Vigorously shake 1 minute daily for 3 weeks. Strain the tincture into a new jar, label, and store in a cool, dark place.

DOTTED BLAZINGSTAR
Liatris punctata

Liatris punctata
Panayoti Kelaidis © Denver Botanic Gardens

Liatris punctata
Jen Toews

Also called: Cachana, dotted gayfeather, gayfeather, rattlesnake master, snakeroot

Related species: *L. lancifolia, L. ligulistylis*

Parts used: Root

Cautions: None known

Season: August to September. Harvest the root in the fall after the first frost.

Habitat and range: Found in prairies and open meadows from plains to foothills throughout the Great Plains and Rocky Mountain region of North America

Description: Erect perennial with unbranched stems, growing to 60 centimeters tall. Several stems bear narrow, crowded heads with light purple flowers arranged in slender wands. Alternate linear leaves 2–4 centimeters long crowd the stem and are dotted. Purple flowers, about 15 millimeters high, contain 4–6 disc florets and appear feathery. Fruits are hairy 10-ribbed achenes, with feathery bristles.

Constituents: Punctatin, eupatilin, amabiline, liatripunctin, otosenine

Medicinal actions: Diuretic, digestive, anti-inflammatory

Cultivation: Prefers well-draining, sandy soil and full sun. This drought-resistant plant attracts butterflies and birds. Blooms late summer to fall. Zones 4–9

The taproot of *Liatris punctata* can grow to depths of 4 meters in prairie soils of North America. This root contains inulin, a valuable indigestible starch which passes through the digestive system, providing food for gut bacteria and also serving as a tonic for the kidneys and liver. The Kiowa dig up the massive root in the springtime, roast it over a fire, and then consume the nutritious food. The flavor is said to be similar to carrot or parsnip. The leaves and buds of *Liatris* are also edible, but are considered more of an emergency food. Medicinally, Plains tribes use blazingstar to heal a wide variety of ailments including kidney and liver malfunction, colic, and sore throat.

To harness the medicinal properties of *Liatris punctata*, make a strong decoction by chopping up the root and boiling for 20 minutes. This tea can help stop bacterial infections and inflammation of the throat. The strong diuretic properties of the root make this a great remedy for water retention, as it is a strong diuretic. Or one can use dried roots as incense for headache relief and nosebleeds.

PINEAPPLE WEED
Matricaria discoidea

Matricaria discoidea thriving along an urban trail
Jen Toews

Matricaria discoidea has rayless flowerheads.
Cindy Newlander © Denver Botanic Gardens

Also called: Disc mayweed, wild chamomile

Parts used: Flowers, leaves

Cautions: Avoid if allergic to plants in the aster family.

Season: Blooms May to September. Harvest flowers when fragrant and in height of their bloom.

Habitat and range: Grows in disturbed ground, compacted soil, and roadsides from plains to montane in the Rocky Mountains. This native species is found across most of the United States.

Description: Aromatic, hairless branching annual growing to 40 centimeters tall. Weak, branching taproot. Delicate, fernlike leaves are pinnately divided, growing to 5 centimeters long. Yellow cone-shaped flowers with disc florets only. Base of the flowerhead contains overlapping bracts that are lanceolate or ovate. Both leaves and flowers have a pineapple-like scent when crushed or bruised. Each disc floret matures to a hairless, oblong achene that is broader at the top than the bottom.

Constituents: Essential oils (myrcene, b-farnesene, germacrene)

Medicinal actions: Antispasmodic, sedative, anti-inflammatory, febrifuge

Cultivation: Grows well in moderately dry soil, in sun to part shade. Although pineapple weed prefers cool weather, it can tolerate heat. Start from seed rather than transplants. Once established, pineapple weed requires little care and will self-sow. Zones 3–9

Pineapple weed is one of 5 species within the genus *Matricaria*, a group of hardy, aromatic annuals that grow throughout the Northern Hemisphere. This genus includes the popular herb German chamomile (*Matricaria chamomilla*), which is native to Europe and Asia and introduced to North America. The more widespread pineapple weed shares similar medicinal qualities to German chamomile: Both species are anti-inflammatory, have calming and sedative effects, and are considered excellent digestive aids.

Pineapple weed's effect on the digestive system makes it an excellent remedy for upset stomach, excess gas, diarrhea, or to simply calm the stomach after a meal. During illness such as a common cold or flu, like chamomile, pineapple weed reduces inflammation, lowers a fever, and sedates for a restful night's sleep. Pineapple weed was once medicine for pregnant women, the tea drank prior to childbirth to strengthen the body and blood for childbirth. Due to the presence of antispasmodic constituents, this herb can ease symptoms of dysmenorrhea. Pineapple weed soothes skin irritation caused by bug bites or a rash caused by poison ivy. The anti-inflammatory properties within the leaves and flower make it a worthy remedy for itching, abrasions, and irritations. When pineapple weed is in bloom, consider harvesting to make a salve, lotion, or simple wash for the skin.

Indigenous peoples including Inuit, Cheyenne, and Cherokee have used pineapple weed for food for centuries. Several tribes including the Nakota traveled long distances over rough terrain of the Rockies to trade for this herb. Both flowers and leaves are a component of many traditional recipes. Pineapple weed's fruity scent and pleasant taste works well in soups, beverages, and baked goods. This plant also makes a delightful tea, tincture, or syrup.

Pineapple Weed and Witch Hazel Toner

The combination of pineapple weed and witch hazel creates an anti-inflammatory and astringent skin formula that can be used in a variety of ways. The astringent witch hazel can clean wounds, tighten pores, and clean skin, while the anti-inflammatory properties of the pineapple weed reduce inflammation and soothe the skin.

Ingredients:

1 cup fresh pineapple weed flowers and leaves (or chamomile)
12 ounces witch hazel water

Instructions:

Wash the harvested pineapple weed to remove dirt and insects, and then pat dry with a paper towel. Place the herb into a mason jar and pour witch hazel on top. Seal mason jar and shake daily for one week. Strain and store in a cool, dark place.

CUTLEAF CONEFLOWER
Rudbeckia laciniata

Also called: Black-eyed Susan, green-headed coneflower, tall coneflower
Related species: *R. hirta, R. montana*
Parts used: Root, flower
Cautions: Avoid during pregnancy.
Season: Blooms June to August. Harvest the root in the fall after the first frost. Flowers should be harvested at peak bloom.
Habitat and range: Found along streams, in partly shaded forests, and moist and wet areas in the plains and foothills from Montana to New Mexico between 5,000 and

Rudbeckia laciniata
Gary Waggoner © Denver Botanic Gardens

8,500 feet elevation; also found throughout central and eastern North America
Description: Clump-forming upright perennial, branching at the top half with terminal, showy yellow, daisylike flowers up to 8 centimeters across. The large plant can reach 240 centimeters tall and 120 centimeters wide. Stems are smooth. Long basal leaves reach 30 centimeters long with 3–7 large, toothed lobes. The alternate leaves become smaller higher along the stem. 6–12 ray florets surround globular cone with many disc florets. Young cones are green but turn reddish brown in autumn.
Constituents: Aromatic compound, quercetin, flavonoids, phenols
Medicinal actions: Immunostimulant, antioxidant, diuretic
Cultivation: *Rudbeckia laciniata* is a striking perennial that prefers sun to part shade and moist to dry, well-draining soil. This species can tolerate hot, dry summers but may need

supplemental water during periods of long drought. May spread profusely. Divide roots every few years to control spread. Zones 3–9

Native American tribes such as Pueblo and Cherokee include coneflower in their diet. The stems and leaves are eaten alone or incorporated into many dishes. A welcoming vegetable after long mountain winters, young leaves are considered a spring tonic that promotes good health. Stems on the other hand are considered winter food, and eaten right from the earth as a frozen snack.

Rudbeckia hirta
Dan Johnson © Denver Botanic Gardens

The roots of *R. laciniata* have immune-stimulating properties, most likely from the complex polysaccharides that reside in the plant. Cherokee consider this root an important cold and flu remedy, and it has been used this way for centuries. Much like *Echinacea*, coneflower root stimulates the immune system, helping to fight off an invading virus or shorten the duration of the cold or flu. These two genera are closely related and share similar chemical compositions. However, one study suggests that of the two genera, *Rudbeckia* has the higher immunostimulatory activity (Bukovský, Vaverková, and Kost'álová, 1995). Considering *Echinacea*'s presence in the wild has steadily declined in the Rocky Mountain region, *Rudbeckia laciniata* is a worthy alternative. The fresh root can be tinctured with 100 proof vodka or cut up and dried to make a decoction when needed.

Aside from being an immunostimulant, *R. laciniata* has other medicinal applications. As a diuretic, the root stimulates the kidneys to increase the volume of water for excretion without affecting the release of important vitamins and minerals. Like its close relative *Echinacea*, cutleaf coneflower shows antimicrobial activity with topical and internal healing abilities. Finally, both herbalists and medical professionals continue to explore lance-leaf coneflower's antitussive and anti-inflammatory potential.

GOLDENROD
Solidago spp.

Solidago multiradiata
Mike Kintgen

Solidago multiradiata flowers occur in dense terminal clusters.
Mike Kintgen

Related species: *S. canadensis, S. multiradiata*

Parts used: Root, leaf, flower

Cautions: None known

Season: Blooms July to October. Harvest the root in the fall after the first frost. Flowers should be harvested at the peak of their bloom.

Habitat and range: Moist meadows, plains, and waste sites; plains to montane throughout the Rocky Mountains and central United States

Description: Perennial herb growing from rhizomes or woody underground stems. Leaves are alternate, typically lance-shaped, and sometimes with tiny hairs. Flowers in showy, yellow clusters; numerous ray florets surround even more disc florets. Fruits or achenes are typically round, with a pappus of white bristles.

Solidago canadensis ssp. *lepida*
Cindy Newlander © Denver Botanic Gardens

Constituents: Saponins, diterpenes (solidagolactones, elongatolides), phenolic glycosides, flavonoids (rutin, quercetin, hyperoside, astragalin), tannins, volatile oils

Medicinal actions: Anti-inflammatory, antioxidant, analgesic, antibacterial, antifungal, immunomodulatory

Cultivation: Grow in full sun with well-draining soil. Staking may be necessary if plant becomes leggy. If rhizomatous varieties begin to take over, divide plants every 3–4 years. *Solidago* are excellent pollinator plants, attracting bees and butterflies. Zones 3–9

Solidago comes from the Latin word *solidus* meaning "whole" and *ago* meaning "to make" or "to make whole." Perhaps this is in reference to the diuretic properties and its ability to flush fluids and waste from the body. There are over 100 species of *Solidago*, many native to North America and the Rocky Mountains. Native Americans of the region have found several *Solidago* species to be useful as a cold remedy, to heal ailing kidneys, and as a dermatological aid. The flowers and leaves were processed and applied to burns, skin ulcers, and wounds, and even to the scalp to promote hair growth. Roots are blended with tobacco and inhaled, but also used to reduce fever and as an anticonvulsive.

In modern herbalism, the flowers and leaves of goldenrod are commonly used to treat upper respiratory complaints. The flowers are an effective decongestant and help relieve clogged or boggy sinuses caused by pet allergies, hay fever, or a common cold. As a decongestant and antibacterial, *Solidago* is a perfect remedy during the cold and flu season. Many believe that goldenrod causes hay fever; however, this allergic reaction is likely due to ragweed, which blooms at the same time as goldenrod. The pollen of *Solidago* is too heavy to be carried by the wind.

Solidago flowers contain high levels of antioxidants which reduce oxidative damage in the body and can help reduce inflammation. Flowers can be easily infused into honey, oil, vinegar, or simply made into a tea or tincture. One clinical study comparing the antioxidant levels of different preparations of goldenrod flowers (tincture, tea, or decoction) concluded that a simple infusion or tea of the flowers contained the highest amounts of antioxidants (Apáti et al., 2003). An infusion of the flowers not only acts as a diuretic, but also contains antiseptic compounds that may relieve symptoms of bladder infection or UTI. An oil infused with goldenrod flowers can be applied to arthritic joints, bruises, or sore muscles. A goldenrod-infused vinegar captures those valuable antioxidants and can easily be incorporated into salad dressings, marinades, and tonics.

Goldenrod Oxymel

An oxymel is a delicious combination of tangy and sweet due to the ingredients vinegar and honey. It can be infused with a wide variety of herbs, spices, or fruit to enhance the flavor profile. This concoction can be consumed alone or added to soda water to make a tonic beverage, used as a marinade, or as a salad dressing. White or wine vinegar can be substituted for apple cider vinegar.

Ingredients:

1 cup fresh or dried goldenrod flowers, chopped and torn into 1-inch pieces or smaller
Apple cider vinegar
Honey

Instructions:

Fill 1-pint mason jar ⅓ to ½ full with dried or fresh goldenrod flowers. In a measuring cup, combine equal parts honey and apple cider vinegar and mix well. Pour the honey-vinegar mixture over the flowers, seal the jar, and shake well. Shake daily for 3–4 weeks. Strain into another mason jar. Seal and label.

COMMON DANDELION
Taraxacum officinale

Taraxacum officinale is one of the earliest plants to bloom in the spring. Bright yellow flowers quickly are replaced by the forming seedhead.
Jen Toews

Taraxacum officinale
Jen Toews © Denver Botanic Gardens

Also called: Chicoria, lion's-tooth, piss-in-bed

Parts used: Root, leaf, flower

Cautions: Avoid during pregnancy.

Season: Blooms May to August. Harvest the root in the fall after the first frost. Flowers should be harvested at the peak of their bloom. Leaves can be harvested throughout the growing season.

Habitat and range: This introduced species from Eurasia lives in a wide range of habitats including disturbed soil, open sites, and cultivated sites; Alberta to New Mexico and across much of North America.

Description: Perennial herb containing milky sap within the flower, stem, and leaves, growing to 40 centimeters tall from a thick taproot. Leaves are lance-shaped and basal, sessile, and pinnate with sharp, backward-pointing lobes. Flowers are yellow, 3–5 centimeters across, have only ray florets, and grow from leafless, hollow stems. Gray to brown achenes appear after flower; white hairlike bristles form a rounded seedhead.

Constituents: Inulin, lecithin, chicoric acid, lutein, tannins, caffeic acid, terpenes, calcium, potassium, and vitamins A, C, and K

Medicinal actions: Diuretic, nutritive, anti-inflammatory, digestive, hepatic

Cultivation: Many varieties of dandelion exist and can improve soil, attract pollinators, and can be consumed. *Taraxacum officinale* var. *sativum* is a French variety with larger leaves suitable for cooking or medicine making. Grow this variety from seed in full sun (or part shade to reduce bitterness) and in well-drained soil. Plants should take about 90 days to mature. Zones 3–10

Dandelion is a common herb that originated from Europe, seeded its way around North America, and currently thrives in many environments. The whole plant is edible, containing both healing powers and high amounts of vitamins and minerals. Many cultures, including the Native Americans of the Rocky Mountain region, consider this plant a spring tonic. After a long winter without greens and fresh vegetables, the nutritious leaves and roots of dandelion have been consumed with enthusiasm and pleasure. Potential health benefits include reducing inflammation, lowering blood pressure, boosting immunity, and supporting the digestive system, especially the liver.

Historical records indicate dandelion has been used as medicine in Persia since the 10th century. Depending on the region or culture, dandelion was thought of as a blood purifier, liver tonic, and a cleanser of toxins and illness. Dandelion encourages movement and circulation within the body, especially the digestive system. The bitterness of dandelion leaves helps kickstart the digestive system, increasing salivation and secretion of stomach juices that break down food. The leaves and root are a diuretic, improving fluid waste elimination, while returning vitamins and minerals such as potassium to the body. All parts of the plant seem to have an affinity for helping the liver, offering mild stimulation to ward off issues such as liver congestion, fatty liver disease, and some skin issues that stem from an unhealthy liver. Traditionally, the chopped root was boiled and drunk in large doses to help dissolve kidney stones, but much better treatments exist today.

There is no right or wrong way to consume dandelion, and almost every solvent available in herbal medicine can be used as a vehicle for dandelion's medicine. The roots can be pickled in vinegar and spices to improve digestion and increase beneficial bacteria in the gut. Additionally, roots can be tinctured or chopped and roasted to make a substitute for coffee. A tea of dandelion leaves can be quite bitter to some palates, but the benefits are enough to get through a cup. The best way to utilize the leaves as medicine is to eat them. To reduce their bitterness, submerge the leaves in boiling salt water for 3 minutes. Then add them to salads, soups or stews, sauté with butter and garlic, or fry up in fritters. To extract the antioxidants and anti-inflammatory properties of flowers, make a syrup, tea, tincture, or vinegar with fresh dandelion flowers.

Dandelion Flower Syrup

Dandelion flower syrup is a great substitution for agave or maple syrup. It is perfect for pouring over pancakes, sweetening beverages, and meals.

Ingredients:

3 cups water
2 cups fresh, organic dandelion flower petals, cleaned and free of pollutants
½ lemon, chopped
2½ cups organic cane sugar

½ cup honey
Pinch of cinnamon

Instructions:

In a large pan, combine dandelion petals, water, and chopped lemon (with peel) over high heat. Bring to a boil and turn heat off. Cover and let steep for 8 hours or more. Strain the dandelion lemon infusion, squeezing out all the tea from the flowers. In a saucepan combine dandelion lemon infusion, sugar, honey, and cinnamon. Simmer over low heat for 1 hour, stirring occasionally, until syrup is thick or at desired consistency. Store in a mason jar in the refrigerator. Syrup preparations are subject to mold and spoilage, so to improve shelf life, keep cool and consider adding vodka to the syrup to retard microbial growth.

GREENTHREAD
Thelesperma spp.

Also called: Cota, Hopi tea, Navajo tea, wild tea

Related species: *T. megapotamicum, T. subnudum*

Parts used: Flower

Cautions: None known

Season: Blooms June to September. Flowers should be harvested at the peak of their bloom.

Habitat and range: Found in disturbed sites, sandy or rocky soil; plains to foothills throughout the Rocky Mountain and Great Plains region

Thelesperma megapotamicum
Mike Bone © Denver Botanic Gardens

Description: Annual or perennial herbs, to 1 meter in height. Leaves opposite, threadlike, and widely spaced along the stem. Disc flowers usually yellow, sometimes reddish brown, and 2–3 centimeters across. Ray flowers yellow or absent.

Constituents: Flavonoids, glycosides

Medicinal actions: Anti-inflammatory, analgesic, diuretic, antioxidant

Cultivation: Grows well in moderately fertile, well-drained soil. Prefers full sun. Sow seeds directly in the springtime when soil is cool. Keep soil moist for 3–4 weeks until germination. Annual or overwintering annual. Zones 5–11

Greenthread has been used by Indigenous peoples of the southwestern United States for centuries. This plant is commonly drunk as a tea, and as a remedy

Thelesperma filifolium
Gary Waggoner © Denver Botanic Gardens

for tuberculosis, respiratory illnesses, and pain. Aside from making a delicious beverage, *Thelesperma* is also a traditional dye plant. The Hopi use several species for a reddish-brown dye that colors woven baskets, textiles, and other handmade goods. Once harvested, the plant is loosely bundled and hung to dry.

Navajo tea is a popular beverage for both recreational consumption and as medicine. The flavor, which is similar to green tea, is described as grassy, smoky, or earthy. The subtle pine flavor pairs well with both mint and citrus. This caffeine-free tea is comforting served warm, and cooling served iced. Greenthread can calm general indigestion and other stomach complaints and is perfect for an after-dinner tea. Based on the Pueblo's use of greenthread tea as a tuberculosis remedy, this herb may provide some relief for respiratory infection and illness. The anti-inflammatory properties can ease arthritis, sore muscles, and general aches and pains. The antioxidants present keep the body healthy and protect from oxidative damage, as well as hasten convalescence. The diuretic action of the flowers supports the kidneys, helping to stimulate these vital organs to release excess water and waste products.

Harvest greenthread by cutting stems 5–8 centimeters above ground level when the flowers are in full bloom. This allows new stems to form and the plant to continue to reproduce. This plant stores well for long periods of time if dried properly. Both the fresh and dried plant can be made into tea, which is traditionally served with honey or sugar.

Summer Iced Tea

This nutritious tea is best served cold. The addition of spearmint leaves helps cool the body on a warm summer's day.

Ingredients:

4 cups water
1 bundle Navajo tea (equivalent to 1 cup of flowers and stems)
½ cup spearmint leaves

Instructions:

In a saucepan, combine water and Navajo tea. Bring to a boil then turn off heat. Quickly add spearmint leaves, then cover the saucepan with a lid. Let the mixture steep for 10 minutes or until cool. Strain the mixture into a quart mason jar and refrigerate or serve over ice.

BERBERIDACEAE/BARBERRY FAMILY

Perennial trees, shrubs, and herbs with alternate, simple or pinnately compound leaves, flowers usually form a raceme or cyme, and the fruit is a berry or drupe

Berberis repens
Jen Toews

OREGON GRAPE
Berberis repens

Also called: Creeping barberry, holly grape, *Mahonia repens,* Rocky Mountain grape root
Related species: *B. fendleri, B. repens, B. vulgaris*
Parts used: Root and fruit
Cautions: High doses may cause stomach irritation. Avoid during pregnancy and lactation.
Season: Blooms May to June. Harvest the root in the fall after the first frost. Fruit should be harvested when tender and juicy.
Habitat and range: Found in moist forests, rocky hillsides, and dry slopes from foothills to montane throughout much of the western United States and southwestern Canada
Description: Low-growing shrub with evergreen foliage and erect branches; spreads by rhizomes. Leaves alternate, pinnately compound, and with toothed edges. Leaves glossy or dull, usually green, but turn red and purple in the winter. Yellow flowers in clusters with 6 sepals and 6 petals. Blueish-purple fruits grow to 8 millimeters across.

Berberis repens in fruit
Jen Toews

Constituents: Isoquinoline alkaloids (berberine), tannins, resin

Medicinal actions: Bitter tonic, alterative, cholagogue, antibacterial, antifungal, antiprotozoal, diuretic

Cultivation: A common landscaping plant, Oregon grape grows in full sun or part shade; however, it will benefit from some protection from scorching sun and drying winds. This species prefers moist to dry, well-draining soil. Once established, water sparingly. Zones 3–8

Berberis repens is a medicinal herb helpful to the digestive system and, more specifically, acts as a tonic for the liver. The liver's primary function is to metabolize fats and carbohydrates; detoxify the body of chemicals, alcohol, and biochemical waste products; and produce bile for digestion. A poor diet, lack of exercise, and alcohol and drug consumption can lead to improper function or disease of the liver. When Oregon grape is ingested, its bitter taste not only causes salivation, but the whole digestive system, including the liver, is stimulated. This stimulation encourages liver filtration and detoxification, which in turn promotes overall health.

The root of Oregon grape contains the alkaloid berberine, which has been studied for its wide-ranging benefits on the human body. Berberine has been shown to regulate blood sugar, a promising treatment in the fight against diabetes. Berberine also has strong antibacterial properties, and medical studies suggest that it decreases bacterial resistance to antibiotics and could help in the fight against drug-resistant bacte-

Berberis repens blooms early.
Jen Toews © Denver Botanic Gardens

ria. Due to the presence of berberine, applying a salve of Oregon grape root on first- and second-degree burns helps the skin heal quicker and prevents infection. Finally, berberine shows promise as a heart-healthy compound, improving blood flow to the heart, lowering cholesterol, and reducing symptoms of congestive heart failure.

Considered a cooling herb, the root of Oregon grape is used to ease inflammation and infections of the body. A topical oil or salve of Oregon grape root has been shown to soothe minor infections that lead to redness, itching, or exudation. Ingesting a tincture or decoction of the root can help clear chronic skin conditions such as eczema, psoriasis, and acne. Oregon grape tincture is prescribed for the prevention or treatment of stomach complaints, especially those caused by food poisoning or traveler's diarrhea. Consider a gargle of Oregon grape for a sore throat or gingivitis caused by a buildup of bacteria.

Tincture for Liver Health

A tea of Oregon grape root is not recommended, simply because it doesn't taste good. Berberine and other constituents of *B. repens* extract beautifully with alcohol, so try making a simple tincture instead. This formula, which contains a combination of hepatic herbs, is excellent for promoting liver health and function.

Ingredients:

8 ounces Oregon grape root
8 ounces burdock root
8 ounces dandelion root
16 ounces 100 proof vodka

Instructions:

Place equal parts of Oregon grape, burdock, and dandelion root in a quart mason jar. Pour vodka over the mixture until covered. Seal jar and label. Shake daily for 3 weeks. If plant material expands above liquid, add more vodka. After 3 weeks strain and store in a cool, dry place.

Take 1–3 dropperfuls of tincture daily to promote liver health. Tincture can be diluted in water.

CACTACEAE/CACTUS FAMILY

Mostly spiny succulents, with alternate leaves, photosynthetic stems, and showy flowers with numerous petals

Opuntia phaeacantha with reddish-purple fruit
Cindy Newlander © Denver Botanic Gardens

PLAINS PRICKLY-PEAR CACTUS
Opuntia polyacantha

Related species: *O. fragilis, O. phaeacantha*
Parts used: Stems, leaves, flowers, fruit
Cautions: Large, stiff spines can pierce the skin and are difficult to remove. A second type of spine, called glochids, are small, sometimes appearing soft and fuzzy. These break off upon entry and are difficult to see and remove from skin.
Season: Blooms May and June. The pads can be harvested year-round but should be harvested in the morning for the best flavor.
Habitat and range: Semidesert shrublands and prairies; plains to foothills, from the Great Plains and throughout central and western North America

Description: Low mounding perennial growing to 30 centimeters tall and 3 meters across. Succulent pads are oval, very spiny, and up to 27 centimeters wide. Areoles on the pads have brown fibers (glochids) and spines which can reach 18 millimeters in length. Flowers range in color from magenta to yellow to peach, and are 4 centimeters long with numerous overlapping petals. Fruit is cylindrical, usually brown to red, and spiny.

Opuntia polyacantha flowers can be a multitude of colors beyond the yellow pictured here.
Dan Johnson © Denver Botanic Gardens

Constituents: Vitamin C, manganese, magnesium, calcium, betacyanins, flavanol glycosides

Medicinal actions: Nutritive, anti-inflammatory, alterative, diuretic

Cultivation: Requires sandy, well-drained soil and sunny, south-facing locations. This plant is very cold-tolerant but appreciates dry conditions in the winter. To propagate, remove a pad from the plant and leave it in a dry, sunny place for a couple of days to ensure that the base is thoroughly dry and has begun to form a callus. In sandy soil or compost, this plant will root quickly. Zones 3–9

The modified stems, or pads, are edible after all the spines have been removed, as are the fruits, which are also known as tunas. Both contain large amounts of water, as well as carbohydrates, vitamin C, and minerals. The pads can be charred in a fire, which simplifies the removal of the sharp spines. Fruits can be eaten whole or turned into many food products including syrup, jams, soups, and candies. Fruits are thought of as a refrigerant and reduce fever and inflammation. Herbalists also consider the fruits a lung ally, knowledge learned from Native Americans. Fruits are anti-inflammatory, increase the productivity of a cough, and control excessive coughing.

Opuntia polyacantha grows in the most challenging conditions in nature.
Mike Kintgen

The pads of *Opuntia polyacantha* have several medicinal uses. The flesh can be used for treating burns and inflammation. Cut the pads in half and place directly on the skin or mash up and use as a poultice. Mucilage from the mature pads shows some antibiotic properties. As such, the flesh of the cactus is effective in treating scalds and infected wounds and may stop minor bleeding. The hypoglycemic effect of the pads reduces blood sugar levels, and thus has been studied for their effects on diabetes—particularly type 2 diabetes. Furthermore, the plant has the capability to reduce cholesterol and protect oxidative damage to the heart, due to high levels of fiber and antioxidants. The tunas are much easier to harvest and require less skill but use extreme caution. However, due to the increasing trend of overharvesting of wild cacti, consider purchasing cacti from a local, sustainable source. High-end grocery stores carry fresh cactus pads that have already been processed, spines removed, under the name *nopales.*

Nopales Salad

This delicious recipe compliments a grilled protein such as steak or chicken, or as a filling for tacos.

Ingredients:

2 cups nopales, cleaned, chopped
¼ cup white onion, chopped
1 garlic clove, chopped
2 serrano peppers, diced
1 cup tomato, chopped
2 sprigs of cilantro
1 tablespoon of lemon juice
1 tablespoon vegetable or olive oil
1 teaspoon oregano
Salt and pepper

Instructions:

Cook nopales in boiling water until they become fork tender. Place the nopales in a large bowl; add onion, garlic, serrano peppers, chopped tomato, and cilantro. Mix the ingredients. In a separate bowl, mix lemon juice, olive oil, oregano, salt, and pepper. Combine and mix all ingredients. Serve immediately.

CANNABACEAE/HEMP FAMILY

Trees, climbing and herbaceous plants with opposite or spiraled leaves, often dioecious with cyme inflorescence; fruits are achenes or drupes

Humulus neomexicanus growing in a foothills canyon
Jen Toews © Denver Botanic Gardens

COMMON HOP
Humulus neomexicanus

Related species: *H. lupulus*
Parts used: Leaf, strobile
Cautions: None known
Season: Blooms August to October. Strobiles should be harvested in late summer when fragrant.
Habitat and range: Prefers cool, moist, shaded canyons or rocky outcroppings between 4,800 and 8,500 feet from west and central Canada, to western United States and northern Mexico

Deeply lobed leaves of *Humulus neomexicanus*
Jen Toews © Denver Botanic Gardens

Description: Twining vines that scramble over shrubs, trees, and other support systems. Hops also commonly cascade down rocky slopes. Leaves opposite, hairy on the surfaces, and with 3–7 lobes. Hops are unisexual, meaning individual plants produce either male or female flowers. Female cones, or strobiles, contain 20–50 flowers while male cones contain multibranched panicles with inconspicuous flowers. Female cones are oval, have a floral or garlicky scent, are very light in weight, and form overlapping membranous scales.

Constituents: Bitter principles including humulone, resin, volatile oil, flavonoids, tannins
Medicinal actions: Sedative, hypnotic, antispasmodic, antibacterial, antifungal
Cultivation: Hops are best grown from rhizomes. In the early spring when the ground is workable, plant hops rhizomes horizontally about 6–12 inches deep. Water frequently to promote root growth, but avoid saturation which leads to root rot. As shoots begin to grow, select the strongest ones and support them with a trellis or string; cut back the rest. Zones 3–8

Hops is a medicinal herb with many benefits including sedative, bitter tonic, antispasmodic, anodyne, and antibiotic (Moore, 2003). The sedative properties of hops can be a lifesaver during bouts of insomnia and can soothe a racing heart during illness or stress. A 2012 study conducted at the University of Extremadura in Spain concluded that just 2 milligrams of hop extract reduced nocturnal activity and encouraged restful sleep (Franco, Sánchez, and Bravo et al., 2012). Keep a small bottle of fresh hops tincture by the bedside or enjoy a warm cup of hops tea before bed.

The volatile oils and resins of hops are bitter by nature, and these constituents can promote digestive health. In fact, according to herbalist Maude Grieve, hops contains one of the most "efficacious vegetable bitters available." Not only is hops recommended for digestion after a meal, but the bitterness of hops tea or tincture can help digestive organs like the liver and gallbladder work efficiently. Furthermore, as an antispasmodic herb, hops may reduce and relax spasms in the smooth muscle of the digestive system. The sedative properties of hops (combined with the digestive properties) make hops an ideal remedy for digestive ailments that are caused by stress or nervousness. For these reasons, it is common to see hops recommended as a tonic for the digestive system. Hops can be helpful for much more than insomnia, providing a remedy for a variety of annoyances

Humulus lupulus strobiles
Jen Toews

such as tension headaches, restless legs, or irritable bowel syndrome (IBS).

Much like *Cannabis sativa*, another member of the hemp family, hops is an effective remedy for pain. A tincture or strong brew of hops tea is excellent for toothache, headache (including tension headaches), or pains including rheumatism and neuralgia. Place a hot poultice of hops on the affected areas. To make a hot poultice of hops, stuff a large quantity of hops into a sock or fabric and tie a knot to keep plant material in place. Place the sock and herbs in hot water, ensuring herbs are saturated.

Calming Hops Body Butter

This soothing body butter can be massaged into dry skin as coconut oil is easily absorbed. Calendula and hops help reduce inflammation.

Ingredients:

1 tablespoon dried hops flowers
1 tablespoon dried calendula petals
½ cup coconut oil
1 tablespoon cocoa butter

Instructions:

Mix all ingredients and gently heat until the coconut oil and cocoa butter are melted. Allow mixture to cool completely and let sit for a few days so the oil becomes infused with the herbs. Gently reheat the mixture and strain out all solids and pour into a clean container. Yields 4 ounces.

CAPRIFOLIACEAE/HONEYSUCKLE FAMILY

Trees, shrubs, vines, and herbs have opposite leaves, no stipules, with tubular or bell-shaped flowers

Valeriana acutiloba
Mike Kintgen

VALERIAN
Valeriana spp.

Also called: Tobacco root
Related species: *V. acutiloba, V. occidentalis, V. officinalis*
Parts used: Root, flower
Cautions: May cause excitement in some individuals. Valerian can be difficult to spot in the wild, and is easily confused with wild parsnip, poison hemlock, and several other species.
Season: Blooms July to August. Harvest the root in the fall after first frost.
Habitat and range: Moist, wooded sites, near creeks and rivers; foothills to alpine; Canada to New Mexico and much of the western United States
Description: Perennial herb with 4-sided stems, up to 90 centimeters tall. Basal leaves are present from spring to fall, leaves are opposite, pinnately divided, with coarsely toothed leaflets. Fragrant pink or white flowers in dense flat-topped clusters; resemble carrot flowers. Fruits are ribbed achenes, 3–6 millimeters long with feathery hairs.

Valeriana acutiloba blooms in early summer in montane and subalpine life zones in the Southern Rockies.
Mike Kintgen

Constituents: Essential oils, iridoids, lignanoids, flavonoids, alkaloids
Medicinal actions: Sedative, anti-inflammatory, antispasmodic, emmenagogue, expectorant, anodyne
Cultivation: Consider growing the close relative *Valeriana officinalis*, a native of Europe and southwest Asia, which establishes itself well in a sunny location in the garden. Much of the research and historical documentation available today is specific to *V. officinalis*, making it a worthy addition to home gardens for growing and harvesting for remedies. *V. officinalis* prefers moist, well-draining soil. Water frequently during dry summers, and mulch to retain moisture. Valerian will self-seed; to prevent unwanted seedlings, cut flowers just as the blooms are spent. Zones 4–9

Valerian has over 2,000 years of wide-ranging, documented use throughout Europe. The word *valerian* is derived from the Latin verb *valere*, meaning to be strong and healthy. The Roman naturalist Pliny recommended valerian for pain in the 1st century, a use that is still pertinent today. During World War II, valerian was often recommended and prescribed to edgy civilians of Britain, scared and distraught over frequent air raids. Here in North America, several species of valerian including *V. dioica* and *V. occidentalis* are utilized by Indigenous peoples including the Cree, Navajo, and Blackfoot. Records indicate Native Americans used the root and leaves as a dermatological aid for rheumatism, bruises, swelling, and painful wounds. A decoction of the root was ingested to relieve stomach complaints and respiratory illness.

Valeriana edulis, tobacco root, is native to the Rocky Mountains and Pacific Northwest.
Mike Kintgen

Due to its complex constituents, valerian is a sedative herb, useful for anxiety, insomnia, calming tension headaches, and painful neuralgia. The root is also used to treat epilepsy, gastrointestinal disorders, and ADHD. Tincturing the fresh root immediately after harvesting is preferred as this will prevent isovaleric acid from forming as it dries. Although isovaleric acid is harmless, it has an undesirable smell, often compared to dirty wet socks. A tincture delivers quick and reliable relief avoiding the need to stomach a cup of unappetizing valerian tea. Another method of delivering the sedative properties to the body is through the skin. To promote a restful night's sleep, make a foot bath with valerian tea or make a valerian-infused oil or salve and rub on the bottoms of the feet before bedtime. Compresses of valerian can reduce muscle tension in the neck and shoulders, reduce abdominal pain, and menstrual pain when placed on those localized areas.

Valerian Hot Chocolate

Ingredients:

3 tablespoons fresh valerian root, diced
3¾ cups whole milk
3 tablespoons fresh lemon balm leaves, chopped
3 teaspoons fresh lavender flowers
6 leaves and 3 heads from fresh passion flowers, chopped
Peel of 1½ oranges, diced
1¾ ounces dark chocolate chips
½ teaspoon of vanilla extract

Instructions:

Chop the fresh valerian root to ½-inch pieces, and place in a saucepan with the milk, lemon balm, lavender, passion flowers, and orange peel and gently heat for 5 to 10 minutes. Strain. Pour the infused milk back into the pan, and then add the dark chocolate and vanilla extract and stir until melted. Drink while warm.

CUPRESSACEAE/CYPRESS FAMILY

Aromatic, usually evergreen trees and shrubs with flaky bark, leaves opposite or whorled

Juniperus scopulorum is common on dry, rocky slopes.
Jen Toews

ROCKY MOUNTAIN JUNIPER
Juniperus scopulorum

Related species: *J. communis, J. horizontalis, J. monosperma, J. osteosperma*
Parts used: Leaf, fruit
Cautions: Those who are pregnant or have kidney problems should avoid this plant. Avoid high doses of juniper, which can cause stomach and kidney irritation.
Season: Blooms May to June. Harvest cones in the spring when they are blueish. Juniper leaves and branches can be harvested year-round. When harvesting juniper, scan the base of the tree for fallen leaves and berries, rather than picking healthy branches from the tree.
Habitat and range: Found on dry, open, rocky slopes from foothills to montane throughout the Rocky Mountains and western North America
Description: Coniferous, perennial evergreen growing up to 10 meters tall. Trunks often twisted and knotty, tree bark is thin and shreds with age. Leaves, which grow to the base

of the tree, are scalelike, up to 3 millimeters long, and lie flat against the branch, slightly overlapping. Male and female cones grow on separate shrubs. Male cones are 5 millimeters long and contain pollen. Female cones are blue, berrylike, and contain 2 seeds.

Constituents: Volatile oil, invert sugar, tannins, flavonoids, pectin, resin

Medicinal actions: Aromatic, antibacterial, diuretic, antispasmodic, expectorant

Berrylike cones of *Juniperus scopulorum*
Jen Toews

Cultivation: Grows only in full sunlight. Junipers are very adaptable to both dry and moist growing conditions but will not tolerate any standing water. Junipers are drought-tolerant and make an ideal choice for xeriscape gardens. Zones 4–9

Humans have known about the antibacterial properties of juniper and have used it to clean air and purify surfaces for centuries. Ancient Romans utilized juniper for home purification, and Europeans used it during the plague. In the Rocky Mountain region, many Native American tribes have used the leaves to purify homes and spaces and also to repel mosquitos. Boughs and logs of juniper are steeped in water which is used to clean walls and floors of a dwellings. Juniper continues to be used for similar purposes today.

Medicinally, juniper leaves and berries are an age-old remedy for inflammation and infection, particularly of the urinary tract and respiratory system. This is due to the high amounts of essential oils and flavonoids present, especially in the berries. A teaspoon of crushed berry tea acts as an antiseptic, creating an inhospitable environment for bacteria that can irritate the urethra. A hot tea or steam of juniper leaves and berries is an effective remedy for sinus infections and congested lungs. Other uses include soaking feet and hands in a strong juniper leaf tea to treat fungal infection of the nails. Finally, chewing a few juniper

Thin and shreddy bark of *Juniperus occidentalis*
Mike Kintgen

berries stimulates the appetite, and helps the stomach secrete more gastric juices for digestion.

Juniper-Infused Vinegar

Harness the deodorizing and disinfectant power of juniper with this easy vinegar infusion. This is a simple, effective all-purpose cleaner, great for cleaning countertops, bathrooms, and even laundry. Once the juniper is infused, place the solution in a spray bottle. If the solution is too strong, add water to dilute.

Ingredients:

1 cup juniper berries and leaves
3 cups white vinegar

Instructions:

Rinse leaves and berries and thoroughly pat with a paper towel to dry. Pack berries and leaves into the bottom of a quart-sized mason jar. Pour vinegar over the plant material, filling the jar completely. Shake daily. After 3 weeks, strain out the plant material. Seal and label the jar. Store in a cool, dark place.

ERICACEAE/HEATH FAMILY

Trees, shrubs, and herbaceous plants are typically evergreen, with bell-shaped flowers.

Arctostaphylos sp.
Mike Kintgen

UVA-URSI
Arctostaphylos uva-ursi

Also called: Bearberry, kinnikinnick, mountain cranberry

Related species: *A. patula, A. rubra*

Parts used: Leaf and fruit

Cautions: None known

Season: Blooms May to June. Leaves can be harvested year-round, but fall is optimal. Harvest red berries in the fall.

Habitat and range: Uva-ursi grows in well-drained soil in open or wooded sites from foothills to alpine in the Rocky Mountains and throughout temperate areas of the Northern Hemisphere.

Description: *Arctostaphylos uva-ursi* is a mat-forming evergreen perennial shrub that is 5–15 centimeters tall. The flexible branches are red, brown, or gray, and sometimes peeling. Leaves are alternate, oval, and rounded at the tip, dark green, hairless, and glossy on top. Pink to white bell-shaped flowers grow at the branch tips and are 4–6 millimeters long. Fruits are bright red, thin-skinned, and 6–10 millimeters across.

Constituents: Phenol glycosides, tannins, flavonoids, triterpenes, hydroquinone, phenolic acids, bitter principles

Urn-shaped flowers of *Arctostaphylos uva-ursi*
Jen Toews

Berries of *Arctostaphylos uva-ursi*
Cindy Newlander © Denver Botanic Gardens

Medicinal actions: Antibacterial, astringent, diuretic, anti-inflammatory

Cultivation: This perennial ground cover grows well in rocky or sandy soil that is well drained. Uva-ursi prefers full sun to part shade, and soil that is not compacted. It is a very hardy plant that can tolerate a wide range of temperatures, wind, and drought. Zones 2–6

A. uva-ursi is often found on dry, rocky slopes.
Mike Kintgen

With its glossy leaves and bright red berries, this low-growing mountain shrub is easy to spot while hiking in the Rocky Mountains. Uva-ursi hugs close to rocks, creeps along embankments, and spreads across dry forest floors with its network of roots. The scientific name, *Arctostaphylos*, was derived from the Greek words *Arctos* meaning "bear," and *staphylos* meaning "bunch of grapes." An important plant for many animals, uva-ursi's leaves are browsed by large mammals including elk, deer, and moose, and the red fruit is eaten by birds such as robins. Other animals, including bear, deer, and small mammals, eat bearberry fruit during the winter months when other food is scarce.

This plant is commonly used by Native Americans as a tobacco substitute or mixed with tobacco and smoked. While there is some documentation of euphoric or narcotic effects from smoking blends containing uva-ursi, there is no clear evidence that uva-ursi has any medicinal benefits when smoked. Often, herbs were smoked for ceremonial purposes, with the belief that the smoke carried the smoker's wishes and dreams to the higher powers.

Uva-ursi contains high amounts of tannins which make it a useful ethnobotanical plant. Herbalists use uva-ursi to treat urinary tract infections, bladder infections, and sluggishness of the liver or kidneys with tremendous success. In fact, many cultures past and present including Ancient Greeks, Welsh healers, and Algonquin have successfully used uva-ursi to treat urinary tract issues. This is because the glycosides arbutin and ericolin in uva-ursi break down into hydroquinone in the body, which acts as a disinfectant on the urinary tract. In addition to helping UTIs, uva-ursi is a strong diuretic, stimulating the kidneys to flush out water. A tea of uva-ursi is an excellent remedy for fluid retention and swelling. Uva-ursi leaves work well as a skin wash for wounds, scratches, and weeping conditions. A strong tea of uva-ursi works well as a mouthwash for gingivitis and mouth sores.

UTI Tea Blend

A tea of uva-ursi is quite bitter and lacks enticing flavors or aromas, so it's best to mix the leaves into a tea blend.

Ingredients:

2 tablespoons corn silk
2 tablespoons uva-ursi leaf
1 tablespoon marshmallow root (*Althaea officinalis*)
1 tablespoon goldenrod flower and leaf (*Solidago* spp.)

Instructions:

Place all ingredients into a quart-sized mason jar. Bring 1 quart of water to a boil and pour over herbs. Let the mixture sit at least 30 minutes or until it reaches room temperature. Strain and drink in 8-ounce increments.

DWARF BILBERRY
Vaccinium cespitosum

Also called: Blueberry, grouseberry, huckleberry
Related species: *V. membranaceum, V. myrtillus, V. scoparium, V. uliginosum*
Parts used: Leaf and fruit
Cautions: None known
Season: Blooms May to June. Harvest leaves throughout the summer. Bilberries should be harvested in August and September, when the fruit is purple and tender to the touch.
Habitat and range: Moist to dry forest floors and open meadows from montane to alpine; Rocky Mountains from Canada to New Mexico and throughout the western and northeastern regions of the United States and throughout Canada
Description: Mat-forming, deciduous shrub growing to 30 centimeters tall. Leaves are 1–3 centimeters long, alternate, lance-shaped. Leaves are widest at the middle, toothed at the end, with prominent veins underneath. Urn-shaped flowers are 5-lobed, white to pink, nodding. Blue fruits are up to 8 millimeters across.
Constituents: Anthocyanins, flavonoids, hydroquinone, tannins, ursolic acid, resveratrol, manganese
Medicinal actions: Antioxidant, antibacterial, astringent, nutritive, anti-hyperglycemic, nutritive

The flowers of *Vaccinium cespitosum* are nodding and occur singly, not in clusters.
Mike Kintgen

Cultivation: Dwarf bilberry requires moist, lime-free soil with a pH range of 4.5–6. Does well in full sun or partial shade but needs sunlight to produce fruit. Suitable for rock gardens. Keep sheltered from windy areas and root disturbance. Zones 2–7

There are several species of *Vaccinium*, known as bilberries or blueberries in the Rocky Mountains, and all can be used interchangeably as food and medicine. *Vaccinium cespitosum* is part of a large genus of plants (nearly 450 species) that includes cranberry, blueberry, lingonberry, huckleberry, and other highly nutritional and medicinal fruits. Dwarf bilberry is a common understory shrub, spreading profusely at the feet of coniferous forests of Engelmann spruce and subalpine fir. The aerial parts, both leaves and fruit, have been a dietary staple of many Indigenous cultures throughout the Rockies. Although quite small and somewhat tedious to harvest, the fruits are delicious and worth the effort.

The leaves of bilberry are similar to those of *Arctostaphylos uva-ursi*, an excellent diuretic used to help treat urethritis and UTIs. The compounds found in the leaves help prevent bacteria from binding to the walls of the urinary tract and help flush bacteria through urination. Some medical studies show that drinking bilberry leaf tea can promote a healthy heart and circulatory system by reducing cholesterol, strengthening capillaries and veins, and increasing circulation of blood throughout the body. In Europe, bilberry leaf infusion is a popular herbal remedy for hypoglycemia, reducing excess blood sugar, and a great compliment to modern treatments for diabetes. An infusion of bilberry leaf tastes green and leafy, and is mild on the stomach. Due to the high tannins in the leaf, this tea makes a great remedy for diarrhea.

The fruits make an excellent jam or syrup, and work well in baked goods, but collecting enough for culinary

Vaccinium cespitosum fruiting in mid-July
Mike Kintgen

treats is challenging. However dried bilberries are widely available in commerce and make a great substitute when fresh fruits are scarce. Bilberries contain potent anthocyanosides which give the fruit their brilliant blue and purple color. These compounds possess both preventative and curative abilities for stomach ulcers, glaucoma, cancer, heart disease, inflammation, and general oxidative stress on the body. An ally for the eyes, bilberry has been shown to slow the development of macular degeneration, improve nighttime vision, and slow or prevent vision loss in diabetics. Bilberries also strengthen the collagen within the human body and protect it from oxidative damage. A diet, homemade remedies, or supplements containing bilberry may help the body with post-surgical recovery, autoimmune diseases, arthritis, or even gum disease. Dried bilberries can be added to a tea blend, while both fresh and dried bilberry fruits can be made into a syrup or tincture.

Bilberry Vinegar

This recipe is a simple way to extract the anthocyanosides from the bilberry fruit and incorporate them into a diet. The vinegar can be used to make beverages, salad dressings, or taken by the spoonful daily.

Ingredients:

1 cup dried bilberries
1 quart apple cider vinegar

Instructions:

Combine dried bilberries and apple cider vinegar into a mason jar. Seal the jar, label, and place in a cool, dark place. Shake or stir daily to promote the infusion process. Allow the fruit to infuse for at least 30 days before straining. Store in the refrigerator for up to 6 months.

FABACEAE/PEA FAMILY

Flowering plants with alternate and compound leaves, irregular flowers with 5 petals, and legume fruits or pods

Astragalus drummondii
Mike Kintgen

AMERICAN LICORICE
Glycyrrhiza lepidota

Also called: Wild licorice

Related species: *G. glabra*

Parts used: Root

Cautions: Easily confused with many other species of the Fabaceae family, some of which are toxic. High doses of licorice root can lead to high blood pressure, low potassium levels, and abnormal heart rhythms.

Season: Blooms May to August. Harvest root in the late fall after the first frost.

Habitat and range: Found along streams and disturbed sites; plains to foothills west of the Mississippi and parts of New England, southern Canada

Description: Perennial herb to 1 meter tall that grows in large colonies from creeping rhizomes. Leaves alternate and pinnately divided into 11–17 leaflets. Foliage is glandular and sticky. Yellowish-white pealike flowers are 10–15 millimeters long and grow in clusters, and mature into reddish-brown seedpods. The pods, which make this species easily identifiable, are 10–15 millimeters long and resemble burrs with hooked bristles.

Constituents: Lignin, glycyrrhizic acid, essential oils, flavonoids, coumarins, phytosterols

Medicinal actions: Adaptogenic, anti-inflammatory, demulcent, emollient, antispasmodic, expectorant, antiviral, antifungal, liver protective, antioxidant

The fruit of *Glycyrrhiza lepidota* has hooked bristles on the exterior.
Dan Johnson © Denver Botanic Gardens

Cultivation: Grow licorice from seed, bare root, or as potted plants in full sun and in moist, sandy soils. Deep tap roots are difficult to eradicate once established. Wait 3 years before harvesting root. Zones 3–10

Glycyrrhiza is a Greek word that means "sweet root." The specific epithet, *lepidota*, means "scaly" and refers to the minute scales on young leaves. *Glycyrrhiza lepidota*, American licorice, is similar to the European species *G. glabra*, which is used in candies, cough syrups, and as medicine. However, *G. lepidota* contains less glycyrrhizin, and is more bitter than its European counterpart. Native Americans such as the Dakota and Cherokee have been using American licorice for centuries for a wide variety of ailments such as sore throat, respiratory complaints, diarrhea, and toothaches.

Licorice root is considered an adaptogen and works on the adrenal glands, which regulate cortisol levels in the body. Cortisol, in turn, stabilizes blood sugar, reduces inflammation, and encourages memory retention. Disease, inflammation, and stress can trigger elevated levels of cortisol in the blood, which negatively impacts human health. High cortisol levels are connected to increased weight gain, acne, mood swings, and osteoporosis.

Glycyrrhiza lepidota
Jen Toews

Licorice sustains energy, improves immunity, and ensures an appropriate response to stress.

Licorice root contains over 300 identifiable compounds, many of which positively influence human health. Recent studies have concluded that the saponin glycyrrhizin has anti-inflammatory and antimicrobial properties, which makes licorice root useful for respiratory infections. The demulcent effects of licorice root can help ease a sore throat and a persistent cough. Finally, a low dose of glycyrrhetinic acid, also found in the root, can alleviate symptoms of acid reflux and heartburn.

Licorice root is believed to increase the efficacy of other herbs. Thus, it is common to see a small amount of licorice root in tea blends and tinctures. In addition, since the root is 30–50 times sweeter than sugar it can be used as a substitute for honey or sugar. For these reasons, consider adding a small amount of licorice root to homemade cough syrup or other homemade remedies. Finally, with its emollient effects, licorice works well in homemade salves, lotions, and skin creams.

Calming Tea

Drink this tea in the evening to promote relaxation and reduce stress.

Ingredients:

½ cup dried lemon balm
⅓ cup peppermint
2 tablespoons fennel seeds
¼ cup dried rose petals
¼ cup lavender
2 cups licorice root
8 ounces boiling water

Instructions:

Place all ingredients into a large mixing bowl and mix well. Store in a mason jar, seal, and label. Combine one heaping teaspoon of the tea blend with boiling water. Steep for 5–10 minutes. Strain and serve.

RED CLOVER
Trifolium pratense

Also called: Purple clover, trefoil

Parts used: Leaf, flower

Cautions: None known

Season: Blooms June to September. Harvest flower heads when they are in full bloom.

Habitat and range: Naturalized weed in open meadows, sandy or disturbed soils; found from the plains to montane throughout the Rocky Mountain region and most of the United States and Canada. This plant originates from Eurasia and north Africa.

Description: Widely branched perennial herb growing to 60 centimeters tall. Leaves, 2–5 centimeters long, are alternate, divided into 3 egg-shaped leaflets, with pointed ends and white coloring in the center. Flowers are maroon to dusty pink, forming dense globular heads of up to 200 tiny flowers. Fruits are 1–2 seeded pods.

Trifolium pratense
Mike Kintgen © Denver Botanic Gardens

Constituents: Isoflavones, flavonoids, coumarins, volatile oils, clovamides, vitamins, minerals

Medicinal actions: Nutritive, alterative, expectorant, antispasmodic

Cultivation: Grow in part shade to full sun in moderately moist soil. Seeds can be sown in fall or early spring. Red clover prefers well-drained, slightly acidic soil. Zones 2–10

Red clover contains phytosterols, which are structurally similar to cholesterol. Phytosterols are hormone-like substances that bio-convert in the body to anti-cancer estrogens and other stress-relieving hormones. Studies suggest that people who have a plant-based diet high in phytosterols have a lower risk of lung, breast, and stomach cancer. Plants high in phytosterols are currently under study for their heart-healthy properties. These phytosterols may also reduce blood cholesterol levels.

The many nutrients found in red clover support the female reproductive system. The vitamins and minerals encourage fertility and fortify the body during pregnancy, while the isoflavones, with their estrogen-like effects, can reduce symptoms of menopause including hot flashes, night sweats, and mood swings. Overall, red clover has a balancing effect on the body during the many changes of a woman's reproductive journey.

Trifolium pratense is often found along mountain trails.
Mike Kintgen

The isoflavones in red clover have shown evidence of improving skin elasticity, hydration, and smoothing out wrinkles. Red clover oil is also useful for burns and minor inflammation as well as ulcers and sores. The oil can ease itching and redness that accompanies eczema and psoriasis. Use this extremely versatile oil on the scalp and hair to alleviate dandruff or in a soap to promote soft, clear skin. With the addition of beeswax, the oil can easily be made into a salve or lip balm.

An infusion of red clover is an excellent source of protein, macronutrients (calcium, potassium, and vitamin C), and trace minerals. Think of red clover infusion as food or as a nutritious dietary supplement. Red clover will replenish the body during and after a taxing illness, fill in the nutritional gaps from dietary deficiencies, and keep the systems robust. Use the infusion in place of water—it tastes great and is safe for all ages to consume.

Red Clover Infusion

This method of infusing allows the minerals and vitamins present within the red clover blossoms to seep into the water, creating a nutrient-dense beverage. To ensure the minerals are infused into the water, steep for at least 4 hours.

Ingredients:

1 ounce dried red clover flowers
32 ounces water

Instructions:

Place 1 ounce of red clover in a ½-gallon mason jar. Bring water to a rapid boil in a separate pan, then immediately pour water into the jar, submerging the clover. Seal jar and let mixture sit at room temperature or keep refrigerated for 4 to 8 hours. Strain and enjoy over ice.

FAGACEAE/BEECH FAMILY

Flowering deciduous and evergreen trees and shrubs. Alternate, simple leaves are often lobed, and the fruit is a nut with a single seed.

Quercus leaves
Mike Kintgen

GAMBEL OAK
Quercus gambelii

Also called: Oak brush, scrub oak, white oak

Parts used: Leaf and bark

Cautions: None known

Season: Year-round; when using oak as medicine, harvest fallen branches and acorns before collecting from the living shrub.

Habitat and range: Found on spacious rocky hillsides and openings in the foothills and montane from southern Wyoming throughout the Four Corners states and western Great Plains

Description: Gambel oak is a small deciduous shrub or tree growing in clumps or dense thickets. *Q. gambelii* varies significantly in height, ranging from 3 to 9 meters. Leaves are 7–11 centimeters long and 4–6 centimeters wide, deeply lobed, bright green and glossy

Quercus gambelii in fruit
Gary Waggoner © Denver Botanic Gardens

Q. gambelii thrives on sunny hillsides in the Southern Rockies.
Jen Toews

above and paler below; in autumn, leaves turn red, orange, or brown. Gambel oaks produce acorns which turn from green to golden brown in September. While Gambel oaks can reproduce from the acorns, most reproduce vegetatively from lignotubers, a woody swelling underground from which new stems may sprout.

Constituents: Tannins, flavonoids, triterpenes, phytosterols

Medicinal actions: Astringent, hemostatic, anti-inflammatory, antimicrobial

Cultivation: This shrub prefers full sun and rocky, alkaline soil. Once established, it is drought tolerant. Zones 3–9

Gambel oak is just one of over 450 species of oak growing throughout the world. From mythology and politics to religion and folklore, the oak tree is a powerful symbol of strength, wisdom, and respect, and has been revered by many cultures and civilizations. Many countries including the United States, United Kingdom, and Germany have adopted the oak as their national tree, and it can be spotted on flags and currencies.

A rich source of carbohydrates and high in vitamins A and E as well as manganese and potassium, Gambel oak has been an important food source for Native Americans occupying the Southwest region of North

Inside a Gambel oak woodland
Jen Toews

America. The acorns are gathered each fall, dried, and ground into flour to be used in soups, breads, and even cheese. Although Gambel oak acorns are much sweeter and less tannic than other oak species, they still need to be leeched with water to reduce bitterness and to make them more palatable.

Due to astringent tannins that reside in the bark, oaks have also been used medicinally to treat inflamed tissues, wounds, and minor infections. A strong decoction of oak bark creates an astringent tea that is too bitter to enjoy as a drink but is effective on skin trauma and irritations. Soaking or pouring oak bark tea over a wound will clean the wound of debris, discourage bacterial growth, and will reduce bleeding by tightening the tissues of the skin. Other traditional uses still pertinent today include using the inner bark of *Q. gambelii* as an antidote to diarrhea, swishing a light decoction of the bark in the mouth to stop bleeding gums, or adding to a sitz bath to treat inflamed tissues of the perineum and genitals.

Oak Wash

This highly astringent concoction has many functions. Use as a skin wash to treat minor scrapes, cuts, or sores. Use as a mouthwash and gargle, or drink in small quantities to treat diarrhea.

Ingredients:

1 ounce oak bark pieces (1 inch)
1 ounce yarrow flower (*Achillea millefolium*)
32 ounces water

Instructions:

Place oak bark and yarrow in a saucepan, add water, and bring to a boil. Reduce heat and simmer until the water has reduced by half, about 20 minutes. Strain into a clean jar.

GENTIANACEAE/GENTIAN FAMILY

Family of flowering plants with opposite leaves, and tubular flowers with stamens attached to the petals

Gentiana algida is one of the last flowers to bloom at alpine.
Mike Kintgen © Denver Botanic Gardens

MONUMENT PLANT
Frasera speciosa

Also called: Elkweed, green gentian
Parts used: Leaf, root
Cautions: Large doses of root medicine are toxic.
Season: Blooms June to August. Harvest root in the late fall after the first frost.

Frasera speciosa individuals only bloom once, and tend to bloom en masse.
Mike Kintgen

Habitat and range: Mountain forests and moderately dry open meadows; plains to subalpine throughout much of the western United States

Description: The pale green, robust, and solitary flowering stem of this plant can reach 2 meters tall. Lance-shaped leaves with pointed tips are arranged in whorls of 3–7 along the stem; stem leaves with pointed tips, 25–50 centimeters long. Basal leaves oblanceolate with rounded tips. Flowers with 4-pointed sepals and yellowish green petals with purple spots are joined in a tube at the base; 4 stamens, large anthers, and a central ovary. Flowers grow in clusters the entire length of the stem. Each plant flowers only once, then dies.

Constituents: Not studied

Medicinal actions: Tonic, digestive, laxative, febrifuge

Cultivation: Prefers sun to part shade in well-drained soil, above 7,000 feet. Zones 3–8

Several Native American nations including Navajo and Shoshoni hold monument plant with high regard, utilizing the leaves and root for spiritual and medicinal practices. The Navajo nation smoke the leaves because this herb has the power to "clear the mind if lost." In combination with mullein, the leaves of the monument plant were rubbed on the bodies of hunters and travelers encouraging strength and safe return. A decoction of the root holds claims of being a general tonic for the body, helping to build overall strength and promote well-being.

Although this plant is not commonly used in modern herbalism, it shows promise as a digestive aid. The bitter principles in the root are stimulatory by nature, helping to promote digestion much like a laxative would. The leaf holds similar qualities to the

Frasera speciosa's 4-petaled flowers with purple spots
Mike Kintgen © Denver Botanic Gardens

root, but when ingested has a milder effect. A tea of the leaves can be used for digestive complaints including gas, diarrhea, and gastritis.

PLEATED GENTIAN
Gentiana affinis

Related species: G. algida, G. fremontii, G. parryi, G. prostrata, G. thermalis
Parts used: Root
Cautions: May cause headache if taken in large doses
Season: Blooms July to September. Harvest the root in the late fall after the first frost.
Habitat and range: Moist sites, open meadows, and bogs from montane to alpine from Canada to New Mexico and much of western North America

Gentiana affinis flowers are stalkless, or nearly so, at the top of the stem.
Mike Kintgen

Description: Hairless, multistemmed perennial growing to 30 centimeters with fleshy roots. Leaves simple and opposite, lance-shaped, and 2–5 centimeters long. Blue to purple flowers in crowded clusters are tubular to funnel-shaped, with 5 spreading petals connected with pleat-like membranes; petals sometimes have green to white stripes or spots. Fruits are tiny capsules with flat spindle-shaped seeds.

Constituents: Bitter principles (iridoids), sugars, flavonoids
Medicinal actions: Bitter tonic, digestive aid, immunomodulant
Cultivation: Grow gentian in part shade, in moist, well-drained soil. Zones 3–8

The stunningly beautiful blue-violet blooms of *Gentiana affinis* can be found easily alongside hiking trails that wind through open meadows above 8,000 feet. The root of this plant is arguably one of the best herbs available for digestive regulation. Maude Grieve's *A Modern Herbal* states: "It is specially useful in states of exhaustion

Gentiana parryi can be found growing in montane, subalpine, and alpine life zones.
Jen Toews

Gentianopsis thermalis, meadow fringed gentian, is an annual native to the Southern and Middle Rockies that has 4 fringed petals and lacks pleating between the petals.
Jen Toews

from chronic disease and in all cases of general debility, weakness of the digestive organs and want of appetite." This statement explains the widespread use of gentian root in aperitifs, digestifs, and sodas. These flavorful beverages are traditionally sipped over ice before a meal to prep the body for food, or after a meal to help the stomach settle. Because gentian increases the presence of digestive juices like hydrochloric acid in the gut, it helps break down and process food. Gentian root also works to regulate the digestive system when it is compromised due to nervousness, stress, or illness.

Gentian root is easy to process into tea, syrups, and tincture, but it tastes intensely bitter. Try brewing a teaspoon of gentian root in 8 ounces of water and dilute until palatable. The best vehicle for gentian root's medicine, however, is alcohol. A dropperful of gentian root tincture or bitters is likely enough to get digestive juices flowing. Dilute tincture in water and add bitters to cocktails or other beverages.

Gentian Bitters

Homemade bitters are extremely easy to make and very economical. These work well in both alcoholic and nonalcoholic drinks.

Ingredients:

4 teaspoons orange peel
1 teaspoon gentian root
1 teaspoon coriander
1 teaspoon cardamom
½ teaspoon caraway seeds
4 cups 100 proof vodka
1 cup water
½ cup sugar

Instructions:

Place the herbs in a quart mason jar and add vodka. Seal the jar and store in a cool, dark place for 15 days. Shake daily if possible. After 15 days, strain the mixture into a new mason jar, and save the herbs. Place the leftover herbs in a saucepan and add 1 cup of water. Bring to a boil and simmer for 15 minutes. Stir in sugar until dissolved in the mixture. Strain the warm mixture directly into the alcohol and mix. Seal, label, and store in a cool, dark place. The bitters should last for several years.

GROSSULARIACEAE/GOOSEBERRY FAMILY

Deciduous shrubs with alternate, lobed or toothed leaves along the stem. Fruits are typically fleshy and often edible.

Ribes aureum
Mike Kintgen

CURRANT
Ribes spp.

Also called: Gooseberry

Related species: *R. aureum, R. cereum, R. hudsonianum, R. lacustre*

Parts used: Leaf, fruit

Cautions: None known

Season: Blooms May to July. Harvest the fruits in late summer when soft to the touch.

Habitat and range: Moist woods, open sites, and sometimes dry slopes from plains to alpine. Grows throughout the United States and Canada.

Description: Deciduous shrub; erect or spreading branches with prickles or sometimes smooth. Leaves are alternate, usually with 3–5 palmate lobes. Flowers range in color from white to red, are saucer-shaped or tubular, and sometimes grow in racemes. Fruit is small and round, red, blue, or black.

Ribes aureum fruit in mid-August
Jen Toews © Denver Botanic Gardens

Ribes aureum blooms in mid-spring.
Jen Toews © Denver Botanic Gardens

Constituents: Tannins, anthocyanins, vitamins, minerals, flavonoids, phenolic acids
Medicinal actions: Antioxidant, nutritive, anti-inflammatory, diuretic
Cultivation: *Ribes* species such as *R. aureum*, *R. rubrum*, and *R. uva-crispa* also grow well in the Rocky Mountain region. These shrubs prefer partial shade and moderately moist, well-draining soil. Provide supplemental water in dry climates until well established. Zones 2–7

The genus *Ribes* encompasses nearly 200 species of shrubs that grow throughout much of North America, Europe, and Asia. Many species in this genus bear delicious fruits in the late summer that are prized for their flavor. The less flavorful varieties were once considered emergency food by Native American tribes such as the Ojibwe and Cheyenne. The fruits could be dried and pounded into cakes for a boost of nutrition during the sparse winter months. Many varieties, including *R. americanum*, were esteemed for their taste and nutritional value. Native Americans and European settlers used the collected fruit for pemmican or processed the fruit into jams and jelly. Fruits can also be used for dyeing fabric red or purple, and wood can be transformed into arrows, utensils, and tools. Currant leaves have both diuretic and astringent properties making them a useful remedy for a wide range of ailments. As a diuretic, currant leaves may help stimulate lackluster kidneys to increase urine output. Although water retention can be a minor discomfort caused by hormonal changes or physical activity, it can also be a sign of more serious conditions including heart disease, edema, or gout. A simple tea of the leaves may release this excessive water in the body and reduce swelling. The astringent leaves can be infused in water and taken as a digestive or relief from diarrhea. Gargle a strong currant leaf tea for sore throats, gingivitis, or small cuts in the mouth.

The fruits of the *Ribes* species vary from red to blue or black, can be sour or sweet, and many contain nutritional and medicinal properties. Black currants are loaded with vitamin C, minerals, and high amounts of anthocyanins, which give the currant its rich purple color. Conclusive evidence states that anthocyanins found in black currants may prevent cancer, improve heart health, and reduce oxidative stress on the body. Other studies suggest that a diet high in anthocyanins may reduce the risk of neurological disorders such as Alzheimer's disease while improving cognitive function. Jams and jelly made of black currant fruit not only can be used for food, but can also act as a demulcent, helping to soothe and cool inflamed tissues of the digestive tract. Throat lozenges, medicinal wines, and syrups are other great ways to preserve the antioxidant-rich juice of the black currant. Red currants also make a great addition to salads, baked goods, and as a beverage.

Currant Shrub

A shrub is a cocktail comprised of a vinegar infused with any combination of fresh fruit, sugar and herbs, then mixed with soda water or alcohol. If currants are out of season, try using blueberries, raspberries, or strawberries.

Ingredients:

12 ounces fresh black currants
1½ cups granulated sugar
1 cup balsamic vinegar or red wine vinegar
1 sprig of fresh rosemary

Instructions:

Gently mash currants in a bowl with a fork. Place the currants into a quart-sized mason jar and add sugar, vinegar, and rosemary. Seal the jar and store in the refrigerator. Shake daily for 3–5 days. Strain the mixture into a fresh jar, making sure to squeeze out all juice from the fruit. Taste the shrub and add more vinegar or sugar as needed. This shrub can be stored for up to 6 months in the fridge. For a shrub cocktail, place 2 tablespoons of shrub in a pint glass, add club soda and ice.

LAMIACEAE/MINT FAMILY

Perennial and annual plants with square stems; leaves are opposite and often fragrant

Monarda fistulosa
Jen Toews

NETTLELEAF HYSSOP
Agastache urticifolia

Also called: Horsemint, nettle-leaved giant hyssop
Related species: *A. foeniculum, A. pallidiflora*
Parts used: Leaf and flower
Cautions: None known
Season: Blooms May to August. Harvest the leaves throughout the summer and fall. Flowers should be harvested when they are at the peak of their bloom.
Habitat and range: Found in moist meadows, woodlands, and on sunny slopes from montane to subalpine in southwest Canada to Colorado, and west to California
Description: *Agastache urticifolia* grows vigorously in moist habitats of the Rockies, sometimes reaching 180 centimeters tall. Look for square stems and opposite leaves, characteristics shared by members of the mint family. Leaves are oval, up to 9 centi-

Agastache urticifolia's lavender calyxes are ornate long after the flowers have faded.
Dan Johnson © Denver Botanic Gardens

meters long, coarsely toothed, and become smaller higher on the plant. *A. urticifolia* lacks the feltlike hairs present on *A. foeniculum*. Dense, whorled, spikelike flowers are purple, pink, or sometimes white. Flowers contain 1 long stigma and 4 stamens. The leaves and flowers are fragrant, with an anise-like scent.
Constituents: Volatile oils, caffeic acids, flavonoids, bitter principles, triterpenes
Medicinal actions: Expectorant, mild antispasmodic, antibacterial, antifungal, antiviral, digestive aid, anti-inflammatory
Cultivation: This long-lived perennial grows well in moist, well-drained soil in full sun to part shade. It tolerates poor soils and is an excellent choice for an herb or butterfly garden. This species can grow up to 6 feet tall in gardens. Zones 5–8

The word *Agastache* is derived from 2 Greek words: *Agan* meaning many and *stachys* translates to spikes. Even though it is commonly referred to as anise hyssop, it is technically neither anise, nor hyssop. The taste is sweet, and pleasantly complex with hints of sage and pine. The flowers attract important pollinators such as bees, butterflies, moths, and hummingbirds.

The medicinal benefits of *Agastache* include its use as a respiratory, skin, and digestive aid. *Agastache* does its best work on a weakened respiratory system. During a common cold, bacterial buildup in the body heightens the inflammatory

Agastache urticifolia
Mike Kintgen

Agastache urticifolia overlooking the East River near Crested Butte, Colorado
Michael Guidi

response, causing increased production of mucus and chest congestion. A hot infusion of hyssop is a great remedy for this condition as anise hyssop, like most aromatics, opens airways and lungs. The antibacterial and anti-inflammatory compounds may prevent a cold from becoming severe, or even shorten the duration. Finally, *Agastache* works well as an expectorant, helping to rid the lungs of excess mucus. Because of its antitussive and relaxing effect on the lungs, *Agastache* is perfect as a warm bedtime tea.

Leaves and flowers of anise hyssop steeped in hot water is an excellent topical remedy for skin inflammation, burns, acne, and other minor irritations. And, due to anti-inflammatory and antibacterial properties, an infusion of this plant would work well as an acne wash. Indeed, the skin healing benefits of anise hyssop have been described for centuries. Even the scriptures state: "Purge me with hyssop, and I shall be clean" (Psalm 51:7). Leaves added to a warm bath emit an uplifting sweet aroma which can enhance mood and create a sense of well-being. A hyssop bath also relieves minor muscle aches, sore joints, and bruises. This infusion can be brewed and stored on the shelf for a few days or in the refrigerator for a week.

Anise Hyssop Cordial

Like most plants in the mint family, anise hyssop is a great digestive aid. The leaves and flower heads make a wonderful cordial. A cordial is a simple drink made by combining alcohol like vodka or brandy with herbs, letting it steep for a week or 2, and adding sweetener. This concoction can be stored indefinitely in a cool, dark place.

Ingredients:

3 cups hyssop flowers and leaves
4 ounces vodka
12 ounces brandy
Honey or sugar to taste

Instructions:

Fill a mason jar ¾ full with chopped hyssop leaves and flowers. Combine vodka and brandy and pour over the herb, ensuring the plant material is submerged in the alcohol. Label jar and store in a cool, dark place. Shake daily to mix and promote maceration. After 3 weeks strain and add sugar or honey to taste.

MOTHERWORT
Leonurus cardiaca

Also called: Lion's ear, lion's tail
Parts used: Leaf and flower
Cautions: Avoid during pregnancy.
Season: June to September. Harvest leaves and flowers when plant is in full bloom.
Habitat and range: Found along roadsides, waste ground, disturbed areas; plains to montane; grows throughout much of the United States and Canada. Native to Eurasia.
Description: Perennial growing to 2 meters tall with stiff, square stems. Leaves are opposite, palmately lobed, with long petioles. All leaves have 3 or 5 points, are hairy on the surface and gray underneath. Pink or white flowers form clusters at the upper leaves. The green calyx is ridged and prickly. Flowers are tubular, opening to 2 lips. Upper lip is covered in white hairs, the lower lip has several lobes, sometimes covered in purple or pink dots.
Constituents: Tannins, alkaloids, essential oil, flavonoids, iridoid glycosides, ascorbic acid, limonene

Leonurus cardiaca has verticillate flowers blooming in clusters in the leaf axils that surround the hairy square stem.
Jen Toews

Medicinal actions: Sedative, vasodilator, antispasmodic, cardiotonic, anti-inflammatory, diaphoretic, hepatic

Cultivation: Motherwort prefers well-drained soil and part shade. During periods of drought, keep moist with supplemental watering. This perennial will self-sow efficiently and may need some pruning after the first few years. Zones 4–8

Leonurus cardiaca
Jen Toews

Researchers believe this herb originated in present-day Japan or Siberia, then spread throughout Western Europe and eventually North America. Documented use of *Leonurus cardiaca* in Europe and Asia as medicine dates back millennia, while in North America, *L. cardiaca* has commonly been used as a medicinal herb by the Cherokee, Delaware, and Micmac nations. This complex bitter herb both relaxes and strengthens the circulatory, nervous, digestive, and reproductive systems.

The genus name *Leonurus* stems from the Greek word *leon*, meaning lion, and *cardiaca* draws from the Latin term meaning to treat the heart. And throughout its history of use, motherwort has been associated with healing the human heart, both on a physical and emotional level. This herb contains a complex assortment of alkaloids, glycosides, and bitter compounds which have been shown to improve heart function, especially when it becomes compromised during times of stress caused by anxiety, fear, or sadness. As early as the 15th century, motherwort has been closely associated with the caring and calming energy of a mother. Herbalists today still offer motherwort to patients who show rapid or irregular heartbeat, overstimulated thyroid, or patients who are in a state of shock or are experiencing grief. Motherwort has been clinically shown to produce a hypertensive effect on the heart, reduce heart palpitations, lower cholesterol, and improve circulation.

In addition to being a cardiotonic, the antispasmodic and relaxant effects of motherwort work well on the digestive and reproductive systems. This calming bitter mint has been employed to relax the smooth muscles of the digestive tract, helping to ease stomach cramping or indigestion, especially for indigestion triggered by stress. Long trusted by midwives to assist in childbirth, an abdominal poultice of motherwort leaves or motherwort tea was used to assist with delivery and to prevent infection. Motherwort is also commonly used as an emmenagogue, helping to regulate menstruation and tone the uterus. Today, herbalists prescribe motherwort for headaches, pain, and mood swings associated with ovulation. A tincture of motherwort is best, as the tea can be quite bitter from the high tannins in the leaves and flowers.

Relaxing Tea

A perfect tea for winding down at the end of a long day, this tea blend promotes relaxation and stress relief.

Ingredients:

1 ounce motherwort
2 ounces linden flower
1 ounce chamomile flower
4 ounces skullcap herb
2 ounces marshmallow root
3 ounces hibiscus flower

Instructions:

Place herbs in a large bowl and mix well. Combine 1 ounce of the mixture with 4 cups of boiling water in a teapot or container with a lid. Let steep for 15 minutes; then strain the tea and store it in a closed container. Allow to cool. Drink at room temperature. During daytime hot flashes, drink 1 cup as needed or sip throughout the day.

WILD MINT
Mentha arvensis

Also called: Brook mint, horse mint, poleo mint
Related species: *M. aquatica, M. × piperita, M. spicata*
Parts used: Leaf and flower
Cautions: Avoid during pregnancy.
Season: Blooms July to September. Harvest the leaf and flower when the plant is in full bloom.
Habitat and range: Found in wetlands, wet meadows, and open to shady sites from plains to montane from Alberta to New Mexico; widespread across western and northern United States and southern Canada
Description: Aromatic perennial with glandular, square stems; grows to 80 centimeters tall. Leaves are opposite, lance-shaped, 2–8 centimeters long, becoming slightly smaller up the stem. Flowers, which bloom in clusters from upper leaf axils, vary from purple to white to pink; the upper lip is notched into 2 parts, the lower lip has 3 lobes of equal size.
Constituents: Essential oils including menthol, tannins, flavones, bitter principles

Mentha arvensis flowers open progressively up the stem.
Cody Ernst-Brock

Mentha piperita provides the same benefits.
Jen Toews

Medicinal actions: Digestive tonic, alterative, analgesic, diaphoretic, refrigerant
Cultivation: *Mentha arvensis* grows best in a garden environment that mimics its natural habitat. It prefers part sun to full sun and moderately moist, well-draining soil. Zones 4–7

Native wild mint can be treated much like peppermint (*Mentha piperita*) and spearmint (*M. spicata*), which were introduced from Europe centuries ago. All three species are closely related and contain similar constituents (menthol), but in varying amounts. Menthol is an extremely beneficial organic compound with a variety of medicinal applications including decongestant, antibacterial, topical analgesic, antispasmodic, and refrigerant (body cooling) compounds. While isolating menthol from the mint plant is beneficial, a tea of mint leaves or eating the nutritious leaf provides the body with vitamins and minerals including vitamin A, manganese, and iron (a reminder that the whole is greater than the sum of its parts).

Mint does its best work as a digestive aid and to treat symptoms of indigestion. The discomfort of overeating, overconsumption of sugar or alcohol, gas, and bloating may be resolved by drinking a simple tea of mint leaves after a meal. The relief comes from the menthol, which has an antispasmodic effect on the smooth muscle of the intestines. Furthermore, scientific studies support the use of mint essential oils to treat IBS (irritable bowel syndrome). Finally, due to the tannins present in the leaf, mint is a great remedy for stopping diarrhea and vomiting.

Several mints, including wild mint and peppermint, have analgesic effects especially when concentrated. The cooling chemicals in mint when applied topically seem to inhibit "pain messages" from being sent to the brain. Therefore, a harvest of wild mint steeped in a carrier oil such as coconut oil works on sore muscles and joints to ease pain. For headaches, rub mint-infused oil on the temples, massaging into skin to ease discomfort. Mint oil can also be applied to an itchy scalp or bug bites to reduce irritation.

Wild Mint Sun Tea

A cold infusion of wild mint, or any plant in the *Mentha* genus, creates a clean and crisp brew with less bitterness. Add sugar to this recipe to sweeten, if desired.

Ingredients:

½ cup dried mint leaves or 1 cup fresh mint
½ gallon filtered water

Instructions:

Place the leaves and water into a half-gallon glass jar and seal. Place in a sunny location for 3–8 hours. Strain and refrigerate.

BEE BALM
Monarda fistulosa

Also called: Horse mint, Oswego tea, wild bergamot
Related species: *M. citriodora, M. didyma*
Parts used: Leaf and flower
Cautions: Avoid excessive use during pregnancy.
Season: Blooms June to August. Harvest flowers and leaves in midsummer, when plant is in bloom.
Habitat and range: Native to grasslands and meadows with rich soil, forest edges, and clearings from foothills to lower montane throughout Canada and much of the United States
Description: *Monarda fistulosa* is an unbranched perennial wildflower that forms clumps via rhizomes, growing to 122 centimeters tall. Like most mints, *Monarda* has square stems, herbage with fine hairs, and opposite lance-shaped leaves. When in bloom, *M. fistulosa* is easy to spot thanks to its unique inflorescence: The purple or pink tubular flowers are arranged in a circular fashion and are about 2.5 centimeters in length. The petals have a long upper lip and a 3-lobed lower lip.

Monarda fistulosa flowers bloom in a rounded cluster at the tops of the tall stems.
Gary Waggoner © Denver Botanic Gardens

Monarda citriodora, lemon beebalm, has citrus- or lemony-scented leaves.
Mike Kintgen

Constituents: Aromatic volatile oils including thymol, thymohydroquinone, flavonoids, triterpenes, bitter components, tannins, rosmarinic acid, and caffeic acids

Medicinal actions: Aromatic, carminative, diaphoretic, expectorant, antiseptic, antimicrobial, anti-inflammatory

Cultivation: Grow *Monarda* in moderately moist, well-draining soil in full sun to part shade. Plant where air circulation is good, as this perennial is susceptible to mildew. Deadhead to prolong bloom time. Zones 3–9

Native American tribes including Blackfoot, Ojibwe, and Winnebago seek out *Monarda* for a wide range of culinary practices. Wild bergamot's fragrant leaves and flower petals make a potent tea with a taste similar to oregano accompanied with notes of mint and thyme. This beverage is known as Oswego tea, named after the Native American people in the present-day Oswego, New York, region. Oswego tea became popular during the Revolutionary War when tea was scarce or highly taxed, earning the name "Liberty Tea" by colonists. Tribes of the Northwest gathered *Monarda* leaves and flowers, added them to stews and beans, or mashed them up with berries and meat to make pemmican. Pemmican is a mixture of tallow, dried meat pulverized into a powder along with berries and herbs. If you encounter a patch of *Monarda* on the trail and have the proper cooking equipment, boil up some leaves and flowers for a delicious trail tea. Or preserve the petals in honey or vinegar to use in the kitchen at home.

Monarda fistulosa contains the important constituent thymol, which is a water-soluble and alcohol-soluble phenol with antiseptic and antibacterial properties. In fact, *Monarda* species including *M. fistulosa* and *M. didyma* are North America's source of natural thymol, an active ingredient in some mouthwashes, toothpastes, and natural cleaners. The leaves and flowers of *Monarda* can be transformed into medicinal remedies at home. Brew a strong *Monarda* leaf tea, then use as a mouthwash to keep bacteria at bay, fight gingivitis, ease sore throats, and ease pain from a toothache. Due to the antifungal properties of bee balm, tea is an effective soak for athletes' foot and nail fungus. *Monarda* also eases respiratory complications caused by the common cold and flu virus because it is a diffusive herb, which helps drain fluids from the tissues, including the lungs.

Because thymol is water-soluble, consider making a vinegar with fresh or dried leaves and petals. The vinegar could be used as a daily "shot" or tonic, or even as a base for a salad dressing. Take this infused vinegar a step further by making an oxymel (an herbal extraction of vinegar and raw honey). The sweet and sour mixture can be fortified with medicinal plants to create tonics, cough syrups, or other remedies.

Bee Balm Oxymel

This oxymel is versatile, a great addition to salad dressings and cocktails, or perhaps used as cough medicine or to relieve a sore throat.

Ingredients:

⅓ cup bee balm flowers and leaves
⅓ cup raw honey
⅓ cup apple cider vinegar

Instructions:

Combine ingredients in a mason jar and seal with a lid. Store in a cool, dark place, shaking daily for one month. Strain and store in a sealed and labeled mason jar.

Nepeta cataria in mid-July in full bloom
Jen Toews

Nepeta cataria, in mid-August after flowering, growing in a suburban green space
Jen Toews

CATNIP
Nepeta cataria

Parts used: Leaf and flower

Cautions: Avoid during pregnancy.

Season: Blooms June to September. Harvest leaves and flowers in the summer when plant is in full bloom.

Habitat and range: Found in disturbed sites and populated areas from foothills to montane; found throughout most of the United States and southern Canada. Native to Eurasia.

Description: Perennial growing to 120 centimeters tall with some branching. Stems are light green, square, and downy. Fragrant, felty leaves are opposite, triangular, or oval, coarsely toothed and with visible venation. Upper stems terminate into dense whorls of purple (sometimes pink or white) flowers on spiked racemes, 3–15 centimeters long. Flowers are tubular, 2-lipped, with 5 lobes and 4 stamens.

Constituents: Nepetalactones, essential oils, caryophyllene, thymol, rosmarinic acid

Medicinal actions: Sedative, antispasmodic, carminative, refrigerant, diaphoretic

Cultivation: Catnip can be easily grown from seed. Sow seed in late spring or early fall. Catnip grows best in full sun combined with average, well-drained soil and regular watering. To prevent reseeding, cut back plant after flowering. Zones 3–9

Nepeta cataria is best known as catnip, an herb that causes euphoria in household cats. However, for humans, it's a sedative herb that is ingested or smoked to induce sleep or produce mild mind-altering effects. Catnip contains nepetalactone, an iridoid which is responsible for reducing anxiety, nervousness, and helping to relax the mind. Catnip's best offering may be its use as a hot infusion at the end of the day to help unwind and rest. While this herb may not work well on those suffering from clinically diagnosed insomnia, catnip is a light tranquilizer for children and adults. Always infuse this herb gently, with hot water rather than boiling water.

In North America, the Iroquois, Cherokee, and Mohegan treat gastrointestinal issues and other minor health issues with this herb. Like most plants of the mint family, catnip contains antispasmodic properties which can ease cramping of the stomach, promote digestion after a meal, and stop diarrhea.

If not using fresh, dry this plant by gently tying bundles of stems together and hanging them upside down, preferably in a dark, well-ventilated area. Once dried, remove flowers and leaves from the stem, and store in a paper bag or glass jar. Catnip can be easily processed into a tea, syrup, juice, or tincture and is also used as a poultice, a chew, or smoked like tobacco.

Gripe Water

This homemade gripe water recipe is formulated for fussy, colicky babies that may be experiencing gas, upset stomach, or discomfort from teething.

Ingredients:

2 cups filtered water
2 tablespoons catnip
1 tablespoon ginger, finely chopped
2 teaspoons chamomile flowers
2 teaspoons fennel seed, crushed
1 teaspoon cardamom
1 teaspoon sugar
¼ teaspoon cinnamon

Instructions:

Bring the water to a boil in a saucepan or tea kettle. Place the catnip, ginger, chamomile, fennel, and cardamom in a cloth tea bag. Remove the water from heat and add the tea bag. Allow the herbs to steep for 30 minutes. Remove the tea bag and add the sugar and cinnamon to the tea. Store in a mason jar in the refrigerator for up to a week or freeze into ice cubes.

COMMON SELFHEAL
Prunella vulgaris

Also called: Heart's ease, woundwort

Parts used: Leaf and flower

Cautions: Avoid consuming if taking blood thinning medications.

Season: Blooms May to September. Harvest flowers and leaves in the summer when the plant is in full bloom.

Habitat and range: Grows in moist to wet shaded areas from plains to montane throughout the United States and Canada. Native throughout the Northern Hemisphere.

Description: This stout rhizomatous perennial herb has square stems and branching crowns and grows to 30 centimeters tall. Leaves, to 9 centimeters long, are opposite and lance-shaped. Purple flowers grow in dense clusters; upper lip is hooded and lower lip is 3-lobed and often white. Calyx is light green to red and hairy along the edges.

Prunella vulgaris flowers have a white and fringed lower lip and emerge from hairy bracts.
Mike Kintgen © Denver Botanic Gardens

Constituents: Flavonoids including rutin, vitamins A, B, C, and K, fatty acids, volatile oils, bitter principles, pentacyclic triterpenes based on ursolic, betulinic and oleanolic acids, tannins, caffeic acid, and rosmarinic acid

Medicinal actions: Antibacterial, antioxidant, antitumor, astringent, diuretic, liver stimulant, reduces blood pressure, vulnerary

Cultivation: Grows best in moist, well-drained soil, and in full sun. This species needs consistent moisture during the hottest periods of summer. Give this plant plenty of space since it spreads. Zones 4–8

Prunella vulgaris is considered a panacea herb by many Native American tribes, including the Iroquois. A panacea herb refers to a plant that has a wide range of uses, prolongs life, or is labeled as a cure-all and is derived from the name of the Greek goddess of universal remedy. While no cure-all herb truly exists, selfheal contains many beneficial constituents that make it a well-rounded medicinal plant. Like the common name suggests, selfheal is a trusty vulnerary herb (much like plantain) containing soothing mucilage and astringent tannins. The presence of rosmarinic acid gives this plant its anti-inflammatory and antioxidant effects which may prevent some cancers and heart disease. Selfheal also contains vitamins and minerals and thus makes a nutritious beverage.

Prunella vulgaris
Mike Kintgen

The leaves of selfheal have been used for centuries by many cultures as an astringent for inflammation of the throat and tonsils, to relieve coughs, and to heal mouth sores. A simple infusion of the leaves and flowering tops is recommended for sore throat and cough. In addition, because the cells that line the digestive system are similar to skin cells, selfheal tea can be used to treat GI issues including acid reflux, upset stomach, and diarrhea. A salve or skin oil made of flowers and leaves is effective on burns, skin rashes from poisonous plants, bruises, and minor cuts or wounds. Applying freshly chewed or bruised leaves on an insect bite works well to stop itching. Selfheal tea and skin washes can be made from fresh or dried plant parts. Before infusing the flowers and leaves in oil, dry for a few days to prevent mold growth. Finally, several medical studies demonstrate that certain carbohydrates within selfheal, including prunelline, have antiviral properties and may prevent the proliferations of herpes simplex viruses 1 and 2.

Selfheal Pesto

Not all herbs need to be processed into a salve or tincture to work on the body; remember, food is medicine too. This dip is rich in vitamins, minerals, and antioxidants.

Ingredients:

2 cloves garlic
½ cup cashew nuts
1 bunch or handful of basil
1 bunch or handful of selfheal leaves
3 tablespoons lemon juice
3 tablespoons olive oil
½ teaspoon salt
¼ teaspoon pepper, optional

Instructions:

Blend the garlic and cashews in a food processor; add the remaining ingredients and process until well blended. Adjust the seasoning and add a small amount of water or more lemon juice if pesto is too thick. Refrigerate or freeze for later use.

MARSH SKULLCAP
Scutellaria galericulata

Also called: Common skullcap, hooded skullcap
Related species: *S. brittonii, S. lateriflora, S. nana*
Parts used: Leaf and flower
Cautions: Excessive consumption may cause nervousness or excitability.
Season: Blooms June to August. Harvest leaves and flowers in the summer when in full bloom.
Habitat and range: Moist to wet sites, forests, streamsides, and marshes from plains to montane throughout the Rockies. Common throughout western and northern North America.
Description: Perennial herb growing to 80 centimeters tall. Square stems are delicate, leaves are opposite, oblong, or lance-shaped, 2–5 centimeters long, and sessile. Small purple to blueish flowers, 15–20 millimeters long, flowering in pairs that point in the same direction off the stem in upper leaf axils; covered with fine hairs, lower lip marked white with blue dots, broad and wavy; upper lobe forms a rounded hood. Calyx with 2 lips; upper hooded. Fruits tiny, with 4 nutlets.
Constituents: Tannins, essential oil, menthone, alpha-humulene
Medicinal actions: Nervine, relaxant, anti-inflammatory, abortifacient, emmenagogue
Cultivation: Skullcap is a hardy perennial that grows best in full sun to part shade. Plant skullcap in well-drained soil and keep moist during periods of drought or when temperatures exceed 90 degrees F. Zones 4–8

Scutellaria galericulata
Mike Kintgen

Several species of *Scutellaria* have found their way into Native American medicine, Old European herbalism, and Chinese medicine as a remedial ally for a wide variety of diseases and disorders. Cherokee use skullcap root as an antidiarrheal, as cough medicine during cold and flu, and for kidney disorders. It was once common practice for Cherokee women to drink a decoction of the root as an emetic to expel afterbirth. Considered sacred, skullcap is a ceremonial herb which helps induct young girls into womanhood. The root is also used to regulate the menstrual cycle. European settlers learned to use skullcap from the Cherokee and other Native American tribes in the 19th century, and it soon became a trusted remedy for rabies and nervous system disorders.

Scutellaria brittonii, Britton's skullcap, is native to the Southern Rockies as well as a few counties in Kansas and Nebraska where it is classified as imperiled.
Jen Toews

Skullcap contains several beneficial flavonoids, including baicalein, which have been shown to be highly anti-inflammatory and anxiolytic. Isolation of these compounds was likely inspired by the knowledge and relationship that Native peoples have cultivated with this herb. Today, skullcap is often used to treat insomnia, anxiety, alcohol, tobacco, and benzodiazepines addictions. Skullcap combines well with other herbs which are relaxing in nature including chamomile, California poppy, valerian, or vervain. Many of the active ingredients in skullcap degrade once dried, so use the fresh flowering plant for a tincture or tea immediately or dry in the shade completely before storing.

Sleep Tincture Blend

This blend of herbs promotes sleep and may relieve minor muscle and joint pains, headaches, or migraines. This recipe contains 4 ounces of tincture and can easily be doubled or adjusted to any amount. These tinctures can be purchased online or at a local apothecary. If you have these fresh plants growing nearby, make tinctures of each before formulating.

Ingredients:

2 ounces fresh skullcap tincture
1 ounce wild lettuce leaf (*Lactuca* spp.) tincture
1 ounce catnip (*Nepeta cataria*) tincture

Instructions:

Combine the 3 tinctures in a measuring cup and stir well. Place into a 4-ounce amber dropper bottle and take 1 to 3 dropperfuls as needed.

Fresh Plant Tincture

Ingredients:

1 cup fresh herb torn or chopped
4 ounces 100 proof vodka

Instructions:

Pack the chopped herb into a 4-ounce glass jar. Pour vodka over the herb until it is submerged completely. Seal and label the jar. Shake the mixture every day for 3 to 4 weeks. After 3 to 4 weeks, strain the plant material into a container, making sure to squeeze out any liquid from the plant material. Store the tincture in a cool, dark place or in a dark bottle.

PINACEAE/PINE FAMILY

Trees are mostly evergreen, resinous, monoecious with whorled branches with needle-shaped leaves and cones

A female cone and evergreen needles of *Pinus ponderosa*
Jen Toews

ENGELMANN SPRUCE
Picea engelmannii

Related species: *P. pungens*

Parts used: Needles, pitch (sap)

Cautions: None known

Season: Year-round. Needles and sap can be harvested at any time of the year.

Habitat and range: Grows on cool, moist slopes from montane to subalpine. Species present from Alberta to New Mexico and throughout the western United States.

Description: Coniferous evergreen, growing to 40 meters tall with whorled branches. Tree is pyramidal with a narrow crown. Bark is scaly and light brown or gray. Leaves or needles are 4-sided, 2–3 centimeters long and sharp-tipped. Male and female cones are present on the same tree. Male cones are purple to yellow and up to 15 millimeters long. Female cones are pendulous, with thin woody scales, and red to purple, becoming brown at maturity.

Constituents: Volatile oils, monoterpenes, sesquiterpenes, pinene, limonene

Medicinal actions: Expectorant, emetic, antiseptic, antibacterial

Picea engelmannii growing in the subalpine life zone
Mike Kintgen

Picea engelmannii has downward-pointing cones.
Bryan Lott © Denver Botanic Gardens

Cultivation: Engelmann spruce grows well in full sun, in moist, well-drained soils. Slow-growing evergreen. Zones 2–5

The needles of *Picea engelmannii*, particularly the tender young shoots, have many medicinal benefits. The young needles contain antiseptic properties and can be made into a tea and used as a wound wash for skin infections or as a mouthwash to reduce bacterial buildup. As an expectorant, the tea can be taken internally to treat symptoms of respiratory infections including coughs and congestion, as it helps to expel mucus from the lungs. Due to diaphoretic properties also found in the needles, drinking the tea promotes sweating and may reduce a fever. Other uses of spruce needles include adding them to a bath to soak sore joints and muscles, and using them to make a chemical-free antiseptic cleaner. For the latter, make a very strong tea of spruce needles, strain, and use the tea to wipe down surfaces including countertops, floors, and walls.

Engelmann spruce, like many other conifers, produces resin, which has potent antiseptic properties. Also called pitch, resin is typically visible on a tree's trunk where wounds exist or damage has occurred. It is amber-colored and clear like thick syrup, or reddish orange to yellow and crusted over. In frontier medicine, pitch was used as an emergency plaster for wounds, helping to seal traumatic skin injuries while reducing the chance of infection. Other uses for resin include epoxy or glue for tools, waterproofing wood and leather, and as a fire starter. Once collected, this pitch can be liquefied with heat, then combined with oil to create a spreadable skin remedy for wounds, infections, or skin issues like eczema. The resin can also be dissolved in alcohol such as 190 proof Everclear, diluted with water, and then used as a skin remedy.

Pine Pitch Salve

Use this salve on cuts and abrasions or massage into sore, overworked areas of the body. It is also capable of treating infections and drawing out slivers or other foreign objects.

Ingredients:

1 part clean pine pitch
2 parts extra virgin olive oil
Grated beeswax (1 part grated beeswax per 8 parts combined liquid oil and pitch)

Instructions:

Using a double boiler, melt the pitch in the olive oil until it is mostly dissolved. Add the grated beeswax and heat until dissolved. Pour into jars and let cool before adding lids.

PLANTAGINACEAE/PLANTAIN FAMILY

Annual and perennial herbs with a diverse morphology growing in mostly temperate regions around the world

Plantago lanceolata
Jen Toews

COMMON PLANTAIN
Plantago major

Also called: Broadleaf plantain, great plantain, ribwort, white man's footprint
Related species: *P. elongata, P. lanceolata, P. patagonica, P. tweedyi*
Parts used: Leaf, seed
Cautions: People prone to excessive bleeding or on prescribed blood thinners should avoid.
Season: Blooms May to September. Harvest leaves from spring until fall.
Habitat and range: Grows in disturbed, cultivated ground in plains to montane throughout the United States
Description: Herbaceous perennial with flowering stalks to 70 centimeters tall and 30 centimeters wide. Leaves, in a basal rosette, are oval, up to 20 centimeters long and 9 centimeters wide, with multiple ribs, and smooth edges. Inflorescence a dense spike with many inconspicuous, whitish, 4-petaled flowers. Egg-shaped fruits encapsulate up to 20 very small, dark seeds.
Constituents: Iridoid glycosides, aucubin, allantoin, flavonoids, mucilage, tannins, saponins
Medicinal actions: Vulnerary, expectorant, diuretic, demulcent, anti-inflammatory, antiseptic, hepatoprotective, hemostatic
Cultivation: Sow seeds in full sun to part shade, ensuring soil is moist until germination. Once established, plantain requires minimal care and may spread vigorously. Harvest young inner leaves. Zones 3–9

Plantago major is native to northern Africa, Europe, and Asia, but has become naturalized in many regions of the world. Because their leaves resemble footprints and the plants, which thrive in compacted soils, also followed settlers' wagon trails and foot paths, plantain earned the common name "white man's footprint." From the Old World to new frontiers, this adventive plant, which is packed with both nutrition and healing potential, has greatly benefited humans. Leaves contain vitamins A, C, and K and the mineral potassium, while the seeds are a great source of fiber and can be processed into flour for cakes or bread.

Plantago major growing in an urban park
Jen Toews

Plantain leaf makes an excellent poultice for bug bites and itching skin, as well as inflammation, burns, and minor wounds. Fresh leaves are especially useful and potent, but dried leaves can be useful for making a tea for internal and external use. Plantain is an extremely cooling and soothing herb for the skin, as well as tissues of the mouth, throat, lungs, and digestive system. This is partially due to the phytochemicals aucubin and allantoin. Allantoin can increase water content of skin cells and promotes cell proliferation, while aucubin contains anti-inflammatory, analgesic, and antimicrobial properties. To soothe insect bites, place a fresh leaf of plantain in the mouth and chew into a poultice, then place the macerated leaf directly on the bite. Finally, plantain leaf makes a valuable salve, which can be used to treat ailments from cracked skin, to bee stings, to eczema.

Plantago patagonica, native to Patagonia and much of North America, has hairy leaves, stems, and flower spikes. It has been given the common name of woolly plantain. Jen Toews

Besides being one of the best skin allies, plantain also works well for internal complaints. For example, inflamed or infected areas of the mouth and throat can be healed by plantain tea or a gargle. Fresh plantain juice from young, tender leaves has shown promise in treatment of stomach ulcers. Drinking plantain juice or tea mixed with honey is a great remedy for pulmonary issues such as asthma and coughs. This herb has also been extensively used as a tonic, especially for obstructive diseases of the liver, spleen, and kidneys.

Plantain Lotion

Using a scale to weigh the ingredients rather than measuring them by volume works best. Make the plantain-infused oil ahead of time in preparation for this recipe.

Ingredients:

16 grams plantain-infused oil
6 grams emulsifying wax
75 milliliters distilled water

Instructions:

Add the infused oil and emulsifying wax into a half-pint canning jar. Pour the distilled water into a heatproof jar. Set both containers in a saucepan containing a small amount of water. Turn the burner to medium-low and heat for 10 minutes. This allows the wax to melt and increases the temperature of the liquid at the same time. Remove both containers from heat. Combine the melted wax/oil mixture with the hot water. Pour back and forth between the containers a few times. As the 2 liquids meet and the emulsification process begins, the mixture will instantly turn white. Stir the lotion for 30 seconds then let it cool for 5 minutes, stirring occasionally. Spoon into a glass jar, seal, and label.

POLYGONACEAE/KNOTWEED FAMILY

Perennial herbaceous plants with simple leaves, swollen nodes, bisexual flowers, no true petals

Oxyria digyna
Jen Toews © Denver Botanic Gardens

WESTERN DOCK
Rumex occidentalis

Also called: Red dock

Related species: *R. acetosella, R. crispus, R. obtusifolius, R. venosus*

Parts used: Root, leaf

Cautions: Those with a history of kidney stones and gallbladder obstruction should avoid this herb. Due to the high amounts of oxalic acid, it's best to consume in moderation.

Season: Blooms June to August. Harvest the root in the fall after the first frost.

Habitat and range: Disturbed ground and moist sites in the plains to subalpine throughout the Rocky Mountains. Also native to western United States and Canada.

Description: Upright perennial herb growing to 1.8 meters tall. Leaves with long stalks are alternate along stem, up to 20 centimeters long, becoming smaller upwards; reddish, lance-shaped, and with curly margins. Inflorescence a prominent narrow, dense cluster of red to green flowers, petals absent. Fruits are smooth, brown achenes.

Constituents: Anthranoids, tannins, sugars, mucilaginous polysaccharides, starch, calcium, iron, oxalic acid

Medicinal actions: Tonic, alterative, laxative, hepatic

Cultivation: Western dock grows in a wide variety of soil types in full sun to part shade. It thrives in moist areas and has the potential to self-seed throughout the garden. Zones 4–8

Rumex occidentalis growing in the Aleutian Islands of Alaska
Zeke Smith

The genus *Rumex* is host to nearly 200 species of plants commonly known as docks and sorrels that inhabit almost every region of the world. In western North America, *Rumex occidentalis* is used by Native peoples as a dermatological aid. Yellow dock, *Rumex crispus*, which is a close relative to *R. occidentalis*, can be used similarly. The Nuxalk of British Columbia use this species to treat rheumatic diseases by placing leaves in a sweat bath. Roots and leaves can be crushed and applied to wounds, skin eruptions, and inflammation. The leaves and stems of western dock are edible and nutritious, having a tart,

Rumex crispus, a non-native dock, grows unperturbed in an urban environment.
Jen Toews

Rumex crispus with fruit forming
Mike Kintgen

almost lemony flavor. According to herbalist Susun Weed, dock leaves are an excellent source of bioflavonoids, sometimes called vitamin P. Bioflavonoids support collagen production, helping our skin feel and look good. Bioflavonoids also increase capillary strength, which reduces bruising. Because they keep blood flowing freely, bioflavonoids help prevent strokes. Finally, they help strengthen our immune system to fight against infections.

The large, carrot-like taproot of dock is considered a tonic, capable of treating skin diseases, digestive complaints, and blood disorders, and it helps the liver work efficiently. *R. occidentalis* is an exceptional remedy for skin eruptions, acne, and oily skin. This root, used alongside other skin and liver herbs like burdock and sarsaparilla, can promote clear, healthy skin. The root is a laxative but should be used in moderation to avoid dependence. Due to the high levels of iron in the root, western herbalists often use a syrup or tincture to treat anemia. Western dock also contains anthraquinones, which have been shown to help stop or slow certain types of cancer cells. Dock root has a bitter flavor and is considered unappetizing as a tea by many, so this herb works best as a tincture, a syrup, or in a tea blend.

Yellow Dock Constipation Remedy
The anthraquinones present in dock root have stimulating laxative effects on the digestive system. When making this remedy use 8–10 ounces of water for every 1 ounce of root.

Ingredients:

1 part dock root (*R. occidentalis* or *R. crispus*)
1 part dandelion root
1 part licorice root

Instructions:

Place roots in a saucepan, add water, and bring to a boil. Reduce heat and simmer for 20 minutes. Strain and serve. Drink 3 cups a day for best results.

RANUNCULACEAE/BUTTERCUP FAMILY

Mostly herbaceous annuals and perennials characterized by numerous simple pistils at the center of the flower

Caltha leptosepala
Mike Kintgen

PASQUEFLOWER
Pulsatilla nuttalliana

Also called: Wind flower

Related species: *Pulsatilla patens* ssp. *multifida, P. vulgaris*

Parts used: Leaf and flower

Cautions: From an herbalist's standpoint, this species is therapeutic but should be approached with caution. *Pulsatilla* is toxic in high doses, causing kidney irritation and decreased heart rate.

Season: Flowering April and May. Harvest the leaves and flower at the height of bloom.

Habitat and range: Grows on open slopes and meadows, from plains to subalpine throughout the Rocky Mountains and northern Great Plains and throughout Canada

Description: Low-growing perennial herb to 40 centimeters tall; solitary or growing in tufts. Herbage is covered in silky hairs. Basal leaves, usually divided into 3s with long, slender leaflets up to 10 centimeters long. Stem leaves in whorls below flowers. Flowers are solitary, with 5–7 blueish-purple (sometimes white) sepals; hairy throughout. No petals.

Constituents: Volatile oils, anamonic acid, anemonin, triterpenoid saponins, tannins

Medicinal actions: Antispasmodic, analgesic, sedative, antibacterial

Cultivation: Prefers full sun to part shade and well-drained soil. Attractive in rock gardens and combines well with spring-blooming bulbs and groundcovers. Zones 4–8

One of the first indicators of spring, the cheerful purple blooms of pasqueflower dot open meadows and rocky areas just after snow melts. Pasqueflower (both *Pulsatilla patens* and *P. vulgaris*) is used to treat hyperactivity and to relax a triggered nervous system due to trauma, stress, or anxiety. While studies are sparse, it is believed that the presence of anemonin within the plant acts as a nervous system depressant by lowering heart rate and reducing respiration. This sedative herb is said to

Pulsatilla nuttalliana growing in a dry meadow in the Bighorn Mountains of Wyoming
Jen Toews

bring groundedness and balance to the body and spirit by harmonizing emotions and calming the nervous system. Thus, it is an excellent herb to befriend during challenging life events including childbirth and divorce. Because of its analgesic properties, *Pulsatilla* is effective in treating painful menstruation, irregular cycles, and premenstrual syndrome. Furthermore, ingesting small amounts of pasqueflower tincture may greatly reduce hot flashes and cramps. Heavily diluted solutions of *Pulsatilla* have also been recommended to treat tension headache,

Pulsatilla vulgaris, a European native, provides early spring flowers in a garden.
Ali Schade © Denver Botanic Gardens

migraine, toothache, and earache. Finally, a small dose of 2 to 3 drops in a few ounces of water is recommended to control spasmodic coughs due to asthma, the common cold, or bronchitis.

Pulsatilla Tincture

Try this low-dose tincture for tension headaches, insomnia, migraines, and nerve pain.

Only the dried plant is recommended for a tincture. Make a 1:2 tincture, meaning for every 1 ounce of *Pulsatilla*, measure 2 ounces of 100 proof vodka.

Ingredients:

1 part dried pasqueflower leaf and flower
2 parts 100 proof vodka

Instructions:

Finely chop pasqueflower, place into a glass jar, and add 100 proof vodka. Shake daily for 3 weeks, then strain out plant material. Label and store in a cool, dark place. When working with pasqueflower start with a very low dosage, perhaps 1–3 drops. This is a low-dose herb that is therapeutic in small quantities.

ROSACEAE/ROSE FAMILY

Generally woody perennials and shrubs often having thorns. Most have alternate leaves and stipules at the leaf stalks. Flowers typically have 5 sepals and 5 petals.

Rosa woodsii
Mike Kintgen

ALDERLEAF MOUNTAIN MAHOGANY
Cercocarpus montanus

Also called: Mountain mahogany, hard hack, palo duro

Parts used: Leaf and bark

Cautions: Avoid during pregnancy.

Season: Blooms April to July. Leaves can be harvested at any period during their growing season.

Habitat and range: This shrub grows on dry and rocky hillsides, open areas, or sparsely wooded slopes. Found throughout the Great Plains and American West.

Description: Deciduous shrub, 1–2 meters tall. Smooth branches with alternate, dark green, veined leaves with toothed edges. Bell-shaped flowers are green, with tiny hairs, around 6 millimeters long and 2–6 millimeters wide. Flower with 5 petals, no sepals, 1 pistil, and 20–40 stamens. Tiny seedlike fruits with 3-to-6-millimeter-long feathery tail.

Cercocarpus montanus thrives in the dry garden.
Jen Toews

Cercocarpus montanus in flower
Jen Toews

Constituents: Tannins; little research has been conducted on constituents of this plant
Medicinal actions: Astringent, antimicrobial, laxative
Cultivation: This very hardy, slow-growing shrub and excellent hedge can tolerate temperatures to –10 degrees F. Plant in a sunny to partly shaded area in well-drained soil. Once established, little care is needed. While mountain mahogany is not prone to insect infestation, deer and elk browse this plant. Zones 3–9

The shrub's name, *Cercocarpus montanus*, translates to "tail fruit of the mountains." Late in the summer, a wispy style, which resembles a tail or feather, appears on the fruit. Due to its heavy and hard wood, mountain mahogany is used by Native American tribes to make day-to-day tools including arrow tips and pipes. The outer skin of the roots can be processed to make a red dye for clothing and fabric. The branches, full of leaves, were once clumped and tied together to make brooms.

Like many species of the rose family, *C. montanus* contains high concentrations of astringent tannins within the leaves and bark. Plant tannins help tone, clean, and soothe skin that is inflamed, injured, or infected. A strong tea made of mountain mahogany leaves can be used to treat tender, bleeding, or inflamed gums. For gingivitis, boil a handful of leaves in 8 ounces of water, steep for 10

minutes, and strain. Gargle and swish the tea for 30 seconds to tighten gum tissues. A tea of the astringent leaves may ease gastritis and diarrhea, helping reduce inflammation in the stomach. The Navajo use a decoction of leaves and twigs as a sitz bath, for postpartum recovery.

A decoction of the roots, bark, or leaves can be used in a variety of ways. Many Native peoples recognize the antimicrobial properties of the whole shrub, especially the leaves and roots. The Mahuna have used the leaf for venereal diseases, applying the tea externally as well as drinking to cure discharge caused by gonorrhea. A

Cercocarpus montanus in seed
Jen Toews

decoction of mountain mahogany can relieve a topical infection or be used as a hair and scalp rinse. Finally, the leaves of mountain mahogany are used by several Native American tribes, including the Pueblo, as a laxative.

RIVER HAWTHORN
Crataegus rivularis

Related species: *C. saligna, C. succulenta*
Parts used: Fruit, flower
Cautions: None known
Season: Blooms May to June. Harvest the flowers at the peak of their bloom. Harvest the bright red fruits in the fall once they have ripened and are slightly soft to the touch.
Habitat and range: Well-drained sites, riparian areas, woodlands, and meadows in foothills to subalpine from Montana to Arizona and New Mexico
Description: Deciduous shrub reaching 4 meters tall with grayish branches and stems. Leaves alternate, 3–6 centimeters long and wide, oval, serrated, glossy, and hairless. Flowers are white, 1–2 centimeters wide, and with 5 round petals. Dark purple to red edible fruits form in the fall, are 1 centimeter across, and contain a small seed.
Constituents: Flavonoids, oligomeric procyanidins, triterpene acids, phenolic acids
Medicinal actions: Cardiotonic, cardioprotective, antioxidant, collagen stabilizing, mild astringent, hypotensive, diuretic, digestive, antiischemic, antioxidant
Cultivation: *Crataegus* species are generally easy to cultivate. They prefer full sun to part shade and well-drained but moisture-retentive loamy soil and take 5–8 years to bear fruit. Rust and fire blight are common diseases that affect *Crataegus* species. Zones 4–8

Crataegus rivularis fruit is bright red when ripe.
Jen Toews

Crataegus rivularis fruit will persist on the tree through the winter months until it is foraged by wildlife.
Mike Kintgen

Many practicing herbalists agree that hawthorn is the most trusted herb for building heart strength and maintaining a healthy cardiovascular system. Constituents in hawthorn fruits and flowers, including flavonoids and oligomeric procyanidins, work to increase blood flow to the heart with a specific action as a coronary vasodilator. Deep purple and red pigments on the skin of *C. rivularis* fruit contain these heart-strengthening compounds. Research shows that consuming the pommes, or fruits, will help fortify the heart muscle, thus increasing the force of contraction.

Both flower and fruit work well in syrups, cordials, tinctures, and tea. After harvesting the flowers, dry and store for future use or process immediately, as they will quickly wilt and deteriorate. To make a tincture, add flowers to a jar with 100 proof vodka. Fresh fruits are preferred for medicine making; however dried hawthorn fruits are easily found in commerce as well.

Heart-Strengthening Tea

This nutritious tea contains herbs that are high in antioxidants, vitamins, and minerals. These herbs are known to strengthen the heart muscle, regulate blood pressure, and reduce stress and anxiety.

Ingredients:

2 tablespoons hawthorn berries
1 tablespoon nettle leaf (*Urtica dioica*)
1 tablespoon violet leaf (*Viola odorata*)
1 tablespoon red clover tops (*Trifolium pratense*)
1 tablespoon motherwort leaf or flower (*Leonurus cardiaca*)

Instructions:

Place all ingredients in a French press or a 32-ounce mason jar. Cover with boiling water and let steep 30–45 minutes or ideally overnight. Strain and serve.

WILD STRAWBERRY
Fragaria virginiana

Also called: Virginia strawberry
Related species: *F. vesca*
Parts used: Leaf, fruit
Cautions: None known
Season: Blooms May to August. Harvest the leaves in spring or summer and the fruits in the summer when ripe.
Habitat and range: Moist and nutrient-rich soils of meadows and forests from the plains to subalpine, throughout the United States and Canada
Description: Low-growing perennial which sprouts from rhizomes below and reddish stolons above. Basal leaves are sharply toothed and divided into 3 leaflets, 5–10 centimeters across, green above and pale green below. Flowers are white, 1–2 centimeters across, with 10 sepals and 5 petals surrounding numerous pistils and yellow stamens. Fruits are tiny red berries 1 centimeter across.

Stolons help this diminutive plant, *Fragaria virginiana,* multiply.
Cindy Newlander © Denver Botanic Gardens

Fragaria vesca, woodland strawberry, is native to the Northern Hemisphere.
Mike Kintgen © Denver Botanic Gardens

Constituents: Tannins, flavonoids, phenolic acids, volatile oil, quercetin
Medicinal actions: Astringent, antioxidant
Cultivation: While *F. virginiana* is one of the species that grows wild in the Rockies, other species and cultivars offer similar medicinal benefits and can be grown in your home garden. Strawberries thrive in loose, moderately fertile soil, and require 8 hours of sunshine a day for the best fruits. They prefer the cooler temperatures of spring and fall, low humidity, and benefit from a layer of compost in the spring or an application of fertilizer. As strawberries grow, they send out runners (stolons). If you are treating strawberries as annuals, pinch off the runners so that the plants can concentrate their energy on fruit development. Zones 5–9

While the fruits of *Fragaria virginiana* are irresistible to taste and quite nutritious, the leaves are the medicinal part of the plant. Safe to ingest in any form, they provide a considerable amount of antioxidants. The leaves are also used internally for minor inflammation of the GI tract. Mild cases of stomach upset, diarrhea, and hemorrhoids can be calmed by a tea of strawberry leaves. Due to the acidic nature of the leaves, drinking strawberry leaf tea may cure mild cases of urethritis and UTIs. A tea of strawberry leaves is also recommended for bleeding or sore gums and minor cuts inside the mouth. Externally the leaves make a great wash to clean dirt from wounds. Strawberry leaves brewed in hot water are an excellent caffeine-free substitute for black tea and provide the body with a high concentration of cancer-fighting flavanols.

Strawberry Tops Syrup

Rather than discarding leftover strawberry tops, consider turning these nutritious plant parts into tea or syrup or blending them into a smoothie.

Ingredients:

2 quarts strawberry tops
½ cup granulated sugar
1 tablespoon lemon juice

Instructions:

In a bowl, combine all ingredients, then stir to incorporate sugar and lemon juice evenly. Cover and refrigerate for 8 hours. Add all the contents from the bowl into a blender and blend for 30 seconds. Place a fine metal sieve on top of a mason jar and pour mixture through the sieve. Use a spatula to scrape the bottom of the sieve to extract more liquid. Makes 2–3 cups. Store in the refrigerator.

BLACK CHOKECHERRY
Prunus virginiana var. *demissa*

Also called: Wild cherry

Parts used: Inner bark, fruit

Cautions: Bark and seeds contain hydrocyanic acid which is potentially harmful if ingested; discard seeds.

Season: Blooms May to June. Harvest inner bark late summer or fall and dry immediately. Harvest the fruit in late summer when ripe.

Habitat and range: Grows near bodies of water and in moist, open sites throughout the Rocky Mountains, Great Plains, and northeastern United States

Description: Deciduous shrub or tree, growing to 5 meters tall. Branches are reddish gray to brown in color, and smooth with raised slits (lenticels). Fresh wood and inner bark smell like almonds. Leaves are alternate, lance- to oval-shaped, hairless, finely toothed at edges, and pointed at the tip. White flowers cup-shaped, and with 5 petals, arranged on 15 centimeter-long racemes. Dark red fruits hang in clusters.

Constituents: Hydrocyanic acid, lanthanum, beta-glycosidase, quercetin

Medicinal actions: Astringent, sedative, tonic, cough suppressant

Cultivation: Although chokecherry tolerates part shade, plant in full sun for best chance of full flowering. Prefers well-draining soil but can tolerate clay soils. Zones 2–7

Chokecherry is an important shrub of riparian ecosystems throughout the Rocky Mountains, providing shelter and food for birds, and food for large mammals

Prunus virginiana flowers on racemes
Mike Kintgen

Prunus virginiana in fruit
Jen Toews

such as moose and bear. Native Americans consider this plant a reliable and nutritious food source and an important herbal medicine. Fruits are gathered in the fall, pressed into cakes, and stored for winter. Very astringent when young or raw, the fruits become more palatable when processed with sugar. The fruit can be turned into delicious jams, jellies, wine, and syrup.

Chokecherry bark is utilized by many Native American tribes as an expectorant, anti-inflammatory, astringent, and antispasmodic. The inner bark of *Prunus virginiana* is used to inhibit coughs, sore throats, and minor respiratory infections. Inner bark of chokecherry can be made into a medicinal tea, syrup, or even smoked. Its reliable antitussive effects make it a popular herbal remedy.

This herb is especially useful as a nighttime formula to soothe and cool inflamed lungs. In addition, the bark can slow a rapid heartbeat and balance irregular breathing that occasionally accompanies respiratory infections. In fact, the bark can be used similarly to hawthorn, a respected cardiotonic which strengthens the heart muscles and regulates palpitations and arrythmias. As the hydrocyanic acid from the bark is metabolized in the body, it relaxes the nerves that stimulate coughing. Wild cherry bark works well on its own or in a formula with other helpful respiratory herbs such as osha and elecampane. A cold infusion is far superior to a hot tea of cherry bark, because of the heat-sensitive medicinal constituents in the bark. Due to the astringency of the fruit, the berries can be eaten to stop diarrhea.

Wild Cherry Cough Syrup

Keep this remedy on hand during cold and flu season. This nighttime syrup relaxes the lungs, suppressing a cough, but also acts as an expectorant to expel mucus from the lungs.

Ingredients:

1 tablespoon licorice root
2 tablespoons fennel seed
2 tablespoons elecampane (*Inula helenium*)
12 ounces water
4 tablespoons chokecherry bark
6 ounces honey

Instructions:

Place licorice root, fennel, and elecampane in a saucepan and add water. Simmer until the liquid has reduced to half. Turn off the heat and add wild cherry bark. Infuse for 6–12 hours. Strain out the herbs and add honey to taste.

ROSE
Rosa woodsii

Also called: Mountain rose, wild rose, Wood's rose

Related species: *R. acicularis* can be used interchangeably with *Rosa woodsii and R. nutkana.*

Parts used: Flower and fruit

Cautions: None known

Season: Blooms June to August; harvest the flowers in summer when fragrant and at peak bloom. Harvest rosehips in late fall, preferably after first frost.

Habitat and range: Found on sunny slopes, along hiking trails with disturbed soil, streamsides, and in forests with dappled shade from foothills to subalpine. Wild roses have adapted to many areas and habitats within the Rocky Mountains. *R. woodsii* is also found throughout much of western and northern North America.

Description: *Rosa woodsii* is a deciduous flowering shrub growing to 1.5 meters in height. It is common to see Wood's rose growing in small groupings or thickets. Stems are gray to reddish brown, the prickles are curved or straight and located at the nodes. Leaves are alternate, serrated, pinnately compound, oval, and 2–4 centimeters long. Bright pink, magenta, or light pink flowers can be fragrant, emitting an unmistakable scent. Saucer-shaped flowers are 5–7 centimeters across with 5 sepals and 5 separate petals with many stamens. In fall clusters of bright red fruits (hips) about 3 centimeters long mature. These hips can remain throughout winter.

Constituents: Volatile oil, tannins, vitamin C, flavonoids, pectin, sugars

Medicinal actions: Flower: aromatic, astringent, anti-inflammatory; fruit: demulcent, diuretic, laxative, nutritive

Cultivation: Best grown in a full sun or partly shaded location. Prefers moist, well-drained soil but can tolerate clay or loamy soils. Drought tolerant once established. Zones 3–8

Rosa woodsii
Jen Toews

For thousands of years, humans have successfully captured the intoxicating scent of a rose in distillates, waters, tonics, and spirits. These preparations have influenced perfumery, cosmetics, and improved our health. Tannins in the flower petal tighten and tone the skin, and anti-inflammatory constituents of the flower reduce swelling and inflammation, making rose a cooling ally for skin tissues. Known for her health and beauty, Cleopatra is said to have bathed in rosewater frequently to maintain her youthful appearance. Try the rosewater recipe below on skin ailments such as acne, eczema, minor rashes, or disturbances. Rosewater is also a gentle and effective eyewash for sore, red, or inflamed eyes. An infusion

Rosehips appear in autumn.
Jen Toews

of rose may ease a sore throat, abrasions in the mouth, or inflamed gum tissue. In cases of GI inflammation and diarrhea, steep 10–20 petals in a cup of boiling water, strain, and drink.

Rosehips contain large quantities of vitamin C, vitamin A, and other powerful antioxidants. The nutrients encased in the bright red fruit made this an important winter food source for Native Americans. During World War II when fresh produce was scarce, the government of England encouraged its citizens to consume rosehips. The British Ministry of Food published a rosehip syrup recipe (see below).

The best time to harvest rosehips is after a hard frost. The low temperatures will help soften the fruit and concentrate the sugars. Eat raw for a nutritious snack on the trail, being careful of the firm seeds inside. The tannic contents of the seeds make them useful to treat diarrhea. As a demulcent, rosehips can help ease a cough, calm irritated lungs, and relieve gastric inflammation. They can be processed into jams and jellies, stirred into soups, and used in baked goods. However, a simple infusion of rosehips is the most effective way to deliver the water-soluble nutrients and medicinal properties to the body.

Perhaps the simplest way to enjoy the medicinal benefits of the wild rose is to smell its flower. The heady, floral fragrance alone will reduce stress, enhance the mood, and calm one's nerves. The effects of smelling a rose are both physiological and psychological. If you spot *Rosa woodsii* or its relatives on the trail, take a moment to observe its presence and enjoy the beautiful scent of a plant that has captivated humans for thousands of years.

Rosehip Syrup

A batch of fresh rosehip syrup is high in vitamin C and antioxidants. The nutritive and demulcent properties of rosehips make it a great remedy for coughs and sore throats during the cold and flu season.

Ingredients:

2 pounds rosehips
3 pints water
1½ cups sugar

Instructions:

Mince, roughly chop, or tear rosehips. Place into water and bring to a boil. Reduce heat and cook until half of the liquid has evaporated. Turn off heat and allow the mixture to cool for 15 minutes. Filter liquid through a muslin cloth and return to a pan. Add sugar and boil for 5 minutes. Place into sterile jars, seal, and label.

Rosewater

The anti-inflammatory and antiseptic properties of rosewater make it an excellent addition to your skincare routine. Rosewater can reduce redness, clear acne, and improve skin tone.

Ingredients:

¼ cup dried rose petals
1½ cups distilled water

Instructions:

Place rose petals into pan and add water. Bring to a boil in a stockpot, cover pot, and remove from heat. Allow to steep and cool for 10–15 minutes. Strain through a muslin cloth into a clear jar and label. Store in refrigerator. Use within 1–2 weeks.

GRAYLEAF RED RASPBERRY
Rubus idaeus ssp. *strigosus*

Also called: American raspberry, red raspberry
Related species: *R. deliciosus, R. parviflorus*
Parts used: Root, leaf, fruit
Cautions: None known
Season: Blooms June through August; fruits in summer; harvest leaves prior to flowering
Habitat and range: Grows on dry hillsides, in forests, and along creeks from foothills to subalpine throughout the Rocky Mountains. Also found throughout northern and western North America.

Description: Multistemmed deciduous shrub growing to 2 meters tall. Stems with numerous prickles are usually unbranched the first year and branched the second year. Bright green leaves are pinnate with 3–5 leaflets and have serrated margins. Flowers are solitary or in small clusters, with 5 white petals 5–7 millimeters long. Fruits are red clusters of 20–30 drupelets up to 1 centimeter wide.

Constituents: Volatile oils, pectin, and malic acid in fruit. Tannins, flavonoids, organic acids, vitamin C.

Medicinal actions: Astringent, laxative, refrigerant

Cultivation: Grow in full sun and in well-drained soil. Raspberry roots are perennial, but the leaf- and fruit-bearing canes are biennial. Provides excellent cover year-round for birds and small mammals. Butterflies and other insects are attracted to the blooms. Zones 4–8

Rubus idaeus ssp. *strigosus* in fruit
Jen Toews © Denver Botanic Gardens

Raspberry fruits are delicious and can be enjoyed raw, cooked, or added to jellies and desserts. The vibrant color comes from anthocyanins, powerful antioxidant pigments that are found in many fruits and vegetables and may protect against some cancers, arthritis, and heart disease. These anthocyanins have protective effects, reducing oxidative damage that hastens aging and decay. Ketones present in raspberries have been shown to reduce belly and liver fat. The fruits are packed with fiber, which helps move food through the digestive system and feed good bacteria in the gut.

Raspberry leaf is found in many herbal remedies and tea blends targeting women looking to strengthen their reproductive system, regulate menstruation, or prepare for pregnancy and birth. The leaves contain fragrine, an alkaloid which has been shown to tone pelvic muscles. The leaves fortify the body during pregnancy by offering high amounts of vitamin C, calcium, and iron and minerals such as phosphorus and calcium. Other benefits of raspberry leaf include easing morning sickness, increasing lactation, reducing hemorrhaging, and reducing pain during labor and after birth. Medical studies support the anecdotal evidence that has spanned centuries. For example, several studies involving pregnant women concluded that labor was shortened for those who drank raspberry leaf tea.

Raspberry root is very astringent and, like the leaves, is considered a remedy for diarrhea, as well as a gargle for bleeding gums, or a wound wash. Raspberry roots, stems, and bark contain saponins, which can be simmered as a decoction, cooled, and then poured over the hair and skin to cleanse.

Wild raspberry leaves
Jen Toews

Raspberry Leaf Tea

This recipe is a refreshing summertime drink, high in vitamin C and antioxidants.

Ingredients:

2 sprigs of thyme
1 orange, rinsed and sliced thinly
2 tablespoons dried raspberry leaves
4 cups water
½ cup orange juice
Honey to taste

Instructions:

Place thyme sprigs, orange slices, and raspberry leaves in a 1-liter jar. Bring water to a boil, then remove from heat. Pour water into a jar, then allow to steep for 15 minutes. Pour through a strainer into another jar and add the orange juice and honey to taste. Refrigerate at least 3 hours. Serve chilled or over ice.

RUBIACEAE/MADDER FAMILY

Shrubs, trees, lianas, or herbs with simple, opposite, or whorled leaves, and stipules between the opposite leaves; flowers in a cyme, usually tubular and white

Galium boreale
Mike Bone © Denver Botanic Gardens

CLEAVERS
Galium aparine

Also called: Bedstraw, catchweed, goosegrass, stickywilly

Parts used: Leaf and flower

Cautions: None known

Season: Blooms June to August; harvest in the spring and summer when leaves are young and tender

Habitat and range: Wet areas including meadows, forests, and open sites from plains to montane, throughout the United States and Canada

Description: A low-growing spreading annual having weak, angular stems with whorls of 6–8 leaves. Both stems and leaves have small, stiff, downward-pointing hairs that cling to objects. Leaves are narrow, lance-shaped, 2–3 millimeters wide, and up to 12 millimeters long. Star-shaped flowers are white to green, and typically grow in clusters of 2 or 3 with 4 petals. Fruits contain 1–3 tiny seeds, which are covered in bristlelike hairs that aid in seed dispersal.

Constituents: Iridoid glycosides, alkaloids, phenolic acids, anthraquinone, flavonoids, coumarins, citric acid

Medicinal actions: Lymphatic tonic, antispasmodic

Cultivation: *G. aparine* prefers a sunny location with some shelter from intense afternoon heat, well-draining soil, and a moist environment. Seeds germinate easily and can be directly sown in the fall or spring. The best crop will be in the spring when temperatures are cool and the leaves are young and tender. Zones 3–9

Galium aparine probably received the common name "cleavers" due to the presence of tiny hairs on the stems and leaves which attach themselves to other plants, trees, animal fur, and skin. The aerial parts of cleavers are also known as "bedstraws" because they were once used for bedding and mattress stuffing. Large bundles of this plant were also gathered and woven to make a sieve to filter fresh milk before consumption. The leaves are nutritious and can be used as a potherb; however the taste of

Galium aparine with bristle-covered fruits
J. Richard Abbott

cleavers is too bitter for some. The seeds contain small amounts of caffeine and can be harvested, roasted, and used as a coffee substitute.

Medicinally, cleavers were traditionally used in remedies for skin ailments. As a poultice, the wet pulp of the leaves can be placed directly onto the skin to sooth insect bites and stings. For a skin wash to treat burns and cuts, make a strong tea of the fresh or dried leaves (3 tablespoons for every 8 ounces of water). The Penobscot, Indigenous people of the northeastern United States, consider the leaves of *Galium aparine* to be a tonic for the body. A simple tea can be made from the leaves to strengthen the kidneys and to flush the urinary tract when irritating bacteria causes inflammation or discharge. Use 1 teaspoon of tea for every cup of water and drink 3 times a day.

Cleavers does its strongest work stimulating the lymphatic system, a network of tissues and organs that help remove waste from the body. This system also functions to disperse lymph, which contains infection-fighting white blood cells, throughout the body. Thus, cleavers can help fight infection, flush fluids, and reduce inflammation. A tincture or tea of cleavers can boost metabolism and kick the feeling of sluggishness. This is an excellent springtime tonic herb, symbolic of movement, awakening, and cleansing.

Cleavers Juice

The leaves of fresh *G. aparine* are highly nutritious and make a refreshing springtime drink. Use a high-quality blender to coerce the nutrients out of the leaves and into the water. Freely experiment with this recipe by adding or substituting other spring greens like dandelion leaf, nettles, or watercress.

Ingredients:

3 cups fresh cleavers' leaves, packed
4 cups cold water
1-inch piece peeled ginger root

Instructions:

Place all ingredients in a blender. Mix the leaves, root, and water on the highest setting for 20–30 seconds until smooth and frothy. Drink immediately. If the consistency is gritty and unappealing, filter the juice through a sieve to remove plant material.

SALICACEAE/WILLOW FAMILY
Trees and shrubs with simple, alternate leaves and unisexual flowers

Populus tremuloides, quaking aspen, is the emblematic deciduous tree of the Rocky Mountains, especially in autumn.
Mike Kintgen

BALSAM POPLAR
Populus balsamifera

Also called: Black cottonwood
Related species: *P. alba, P. angustifolia*
Parts used: Leaf buds, bark
Cautions: None known

Season: Blooms April to May; harvest the leaf buds in the springtime and the inner bark in the spring or fall

Habitat and range: Grows throughout much of the northern United States and Canada in moist to wet sites near rivers and lakes in the foothills to subalpine

Description: Deciduous tree, growing to 25 meters tall. Trunk can reach 1 meter in diameter and is dark gray and deeply grooved. Alternate leaves, 5–12 centimeters long, are oval with pointed tips, green above, and paler and veined below. Flowers form on

Populus balsamifera has dark gray and deeply grooved bark.
Mike Kintgen

catkins up to 8 centimeters long; male and female catkins are on separate trees. Fruits grow into egg-shaped green catkins, then open to release tiny seeds with soft white hairs which aid in wind dispersal.

Constituents: Aromatic terpenes, sesquiterpenoids, glycosides (salicin, populin)

Medicinal actions: Antiseptic, analgesic, expectorant, diuretic, tonic, stimulant

Cultivation: Prefers a sunny, moist location and sandy soil. Zones 2–9

Balsamifera translates to "balsam bearing," referring to the fragrant resin that is present on the leaf buds each spring. The formation of the resinous leaf buds usually coincides with spring windstorms that knock large branches to the ground, allowing for easy harvesting without harming the tree. Balsam, which exudes from various trees and shrubs, has been historically used as a base for cosmetics, medicine, and fragrances. The spring buds, which contain the compounds populin and salicin, are prized medicine. These compounds are present in many members of the willow family including *P. balsamifera*, and can ease pain, inflammation, and fever. When ingested, salicin will metabolize into salicylic acid, acting much like over-the-counter medicine aspirin. Balsam buds are a strong analgesic and were often used in sweat baths or soaks for rheumatic pain or infused in oil and applied to bruises, sprains, and other injuries. Leaves and branches contain the same pain-relieving compounds as the buds. The Nuxalk tribe of British Columbia use the fallen leaves and twigs of the black cottonwood in a hot-water soak to ease pain and inflammation.

Populus balsamifera leaves
Mike Kintgen

The aromatic resin from the leaf buds also provides strong expectorant action for the lungs during respiratory and allergy season. A tea of the buds relieves congestion in the lungs caused by respiratory illness. The buds can be boiled to create vapors, which are an effective expectorant when inhaled. A salve of black cottonwood buds is also known as "Balm of Gilead." This balm can be rubbed on the chest or even inside nostrils allowing the vapors to work their way through the respiratory system providing immediate relief and healing.

Balm of Gilead Oil

Massage this oil on sore muscles, inflamed joints, or on other body aches. To relieve chest congestion, massage externally before sleep. This recipe does not include exact measurements because harvest may be limited. Use spring buds before they have begun to open, when the amount of aromatic oil-soluble resin is relatively less compared to the amount of water and water-soluble materials.

Instructions:

Fill a mason jar half full with buds, and pour olive oil to fill ¾ of the jar. Shake the jar every few days and store in a cool, dark place. Check to make sure buds are submerged in oil, and if they are not, add more oil. After 6 weeks, strain into a clear jar, and label.

WILLOW
Salix spp.

Related species: S. candida, S. exigua, S. geyeriana, S. purpurea
Parts used: Inner bark
Cautions: Avoid if hypersensitive to salicylates. Willow bark has varying amounts of salicin and is difficult to standardize when making homemade remedies.
Season: Blooms from April to June; harvest bark in spring
Habitat and range: Found in moist environments and open meadows from plains to alpine throughout the United States and Canada
Description: Deciduous trees and shrubs. Leaves are alternate and typically elongated. Leaf buds are lateral (growing along the stem) and never terminal (growing at the end of the stem). Dioecious male and female flowers appear as catkins in early spring, often before the leaves emerge.
Constituents: Salicin (concentration depends on season and species), flavonoids, tannins, phenolic acids
Medicinal actions: Anti-inflammatory, analgesic, astringent
Cultivation: Willows grow in fertile, well-drained soil. Plant in full sun to part shade. Willows can tolerate high temperatures and periods of drought, but supplement with water or plant in partial shade to protect from the afternoon sun. Zones vary based on species.

The leaves of *Salix* spp. are often elongated.
Jen Toews

Catkins of *Salix drummondii*
Mike Kintgen

Members of Salicaceae include aspen, cottonwood, poplar, and willow. These shrubs and trees are considered healers of the earth and are typically the first plants to move into a landscape altered by fire or severe erosive events. Willows stabilize soil, provide food for animals, and have been an important plant for humans for centuries. Willow twigs were made into baskets, fish traps, and other tools as early as 8,000 BC, and the use of willow as a medicine dates back millennia.

The sap within the branches and twigs of willow is rich in the glycosides salicin and populin, as well as tannins. Salicin and populin are anti-inflammatory compounds that have been shown to reduce fever and relieve pain. When salicin is ingested, it moves through the digestive system and converts into salicylic acid. The isolation of salicylic acid in the 19th century by chemists helped pave the way for the creation of aspirin, a medication used to treat pain, fever, and inflammation. It is important to note that willow bark also contains a small amount of salicin. It is likely that the high flavonoid and polyphenol content, as well as other complex components of willow bark, contribute to the anti-inflammatory effect. Unlike synthetically produced aspirin, willow bark does not seem to irritate the gastrointestinal mucosa.

Willow bark can ease rheumatic joint pain, headaches, migraines, and thin the blood. Feverish states and symptoms of cold and flu can be eased with willow bark. Due to its tannic content, willow bark makes a worthy astringent for diarrhea, bladder

Salix spp. growing in a drainage in Middle Park, Colorado
Jen Toews

complaints, and inflammation of the urethra. There are several ways to prepare willow bark for consumption: make a tincture using 100 proof vodka, make a tea, or mix in a tea blend. Due to the presence of salicin, willow bark is also an excellent herb for the skin. The salicin in willow exfoliates dead and dry skin cells and its anti-inflammatory properties help clear up acne and blemishes. Make fresh tea of willow bark and apply gently to the skin. For a more shelf-stable skin-care product, infuse willow bark in witch hazel.

Willow Bark Toner

This recipe works well for oily skin, as well as acne-prone skin.

Ingredients:

1 tablespoon willow bark
⅓ cup boiling water
2 tablespoons witch hazel
1 tablespoon vegetable glycerin

Instructions:

Make a tea of willow bark, letting the herb sit for 15 minutes before straining. While the tea is brewing, combine the other ingredients in a pint-sized mason jar. Stir in hot tea. Store in an amber dropper bottle with a spray top. The toner should keep for 1–2 weeks.

SCROPHULARIACEAE/FIGWORT FAMILY

Annual and perennial herbs with irregular, bilateral flowers containing 5 united petals, 2 lipped with 2 lobes pointed up and 3 pointing down

Scrophularia macrantha, a New Mexico native, is a favored flower of hummingbirds and bees.
Mike Kintgen

COMMON MULLEIN
Verbascum thapsus

Also called: Candlewick plant, cowboy's toilet paper, great mullein, velvet-dock, woolly mullein

Parts used: Root, leaf, flower

Cautions: The woolly hairs of mullein can be irritating to the mouth and throat. Filter or strain infusion before consumption.

Season: Blooms June to August. Harvest flowers in summer at peak bloom. Harvest leaves throughout the growing season.

Habitat and range: Grows in meadows and disturbed sites from plains to subalpine; found from Canada to New Mexico, and throughout the United States

Verbascum thapsus first-year basal rosette
Jen Toews © Denver Botanic Gardens

Description: Woolly biennial with a single stem to 200 centimeters tall from taproot. During the first year a basal rosette emerges and sometimes persists through the second year. Basal leaves lance-shaped, to 40 centimeters long. Second year's stalk forms, leaves alternate. Dense yellow flowers, saucer-shaped, with 5 petals, bloom spirally up the tall stem. Fruits are round, furry capsules to 10 millimeters long.

Constituents: Saponins, iridoids, glycosides, flavonoids, vitamin C, minerals

Medicinal actions: Antibacterial, anti-inflammatory, antioxidant, expectorant, antispasmodic, emollient, demulcent

Cultivation: Common mullein is found in full sun, well-draining soil and can tolerate periods of drought. *Verbascum thapsus* is considered a noxious weed in many regions of the United States and should not be grown. However, there are other species and cultivars of mullein, including *V. bombyciferum*, that are suitable replacements of *V. thapsus*.

Mullein leaf is a long-established remedy for chest colds, asthma, bronchitis, and other illnesses affecting the lungs and respiratory system. The leaf contains saponins and glycosides which have an expectorant effect on the lungs. The leaves and flowers of mullein contain complex sugars that act as an emollient and demulcent for the skin and mucosal membranes. This mucilage soothes inflamed throat and lung tissue as well as skin rashes, burns, and inflammation caused by bacterial infections. Mullein tea can be especially useful during the onset of a chest cold or infection; when bacteria begins to proliferate, the lungs feel hot, and a fever is present.

Verbascum thapsus second-year plant
Jen Toews © Denver Botanic Gardens

Verbascum bombyciferum 'Polarsommer' provides visual interest in the dry garden.
Cindy Newlander © Denver Botanic Gardens

One isolated constituent within mullein, verbascoside, has shown antimicrobial activity. Historical records prove mullein was an effective treatment for tuberculosis, an infectious bacterial lung disease that has plagued human populations for centuries. Mullein leaf makes an excellent tonic for the lungs, since it contains no known harmful substances and can be consumed over a long period of time. Mullein leaf can also be dried and rolled into cigarettes, then smoked to reduce inflammation and encourage expectoration. One or two puffs is all that is needed for the medicinal effect. An alternative way to take in the smoke is by lighting the mullein cigarette and wafting the smoke toward the nostrils and mouth while inhaling.

Mullein root is a diuretic and its astringency is useful for mild urinary tract infections. Having a toning effect on the kidneys, herbalists turn to mullein root for cystitis, nighttime bedwetting, and painful or difficult urination. Mullein root tincture is a promising remedy for an enlarged prostate as well as strengthening the muscles at the base of the bladder. A decoction of mullein root also helps lungs suffering from dryness or chronic cough and helps encourage a productive cough.

The delicate mullein flowers contain high amounts of antimicrobial compounds that extract well in oil. Lab studies have shown mullein flower's potential to kill bacteria, specifically *Staphylococcus aureus* and *E. coli*, which can cause a wide variety of health issues in the body. Skin ailments and irritations caused by bacteria and inflammation may respond well to the application of mullein flower oil. Massage the infused oil onto eczema and psoriasis spots, rashes, and minor cuts. Another specific use of mullein flower oil is for ear infections, especially those that affect children and pets. Studies suggest a few drops of mullein flower oil into the ear canal can be as effective as amoxicillin. Mullein flowers can also be used in conjunction with the leaves to treat lung infections by staving off infection, sedating lung tissue, and reducing spasms.

Mullein Flower Oil

Dried mullein flowers can be used in this recipe, but fresh flowers, harvested at the height of their bloom, are more potent. If the addition of garlic is off-putting, the flowers will work fine on their own.

Ingredients:

1 cup fresh mullein flowers
2 heads of garlic
2 cups olive oil
¼ teaspoon vitamin E oil

Instructions:

Place the mullein flowers in the bottom of a quart-sized jar. Separate the garlic cloves from the garlic head. Peel each clove. Coarsely chop the garlic and add to the jar. Cover the mullein flowers and garlic with olive oil. Stir gently to remove any trapped air. Seal the jar. Fill a crockpot half full of water. Place the covered jar in the crockpot. Cover the crockpot with a lid to hold in the warmth. Put it on the "warm" setting, or the lowest setting of the crockpot. Leave it for 8 to 12 hours, if possible. Strain the oil into a dark-colored jar to reduce light from hitting the oil. Add vitamin E oil to the infused oil. Label and store in a dark, cool place.

URTICACEAE/NETTLE FAMILY

Herbs, shrubs, and small trees with simple, opposite or alternate leaves, usually with stipules, and many members with stinging hairs (trichomes) on stems and leaves. Flowers are either male or female, and usually borne on the same plant. Fruit is an achene or drupe.

Urtica dioica
Jen Toews

NETTLE
Urtica dioica

Also called: Common nettle, stinging nettle

Parts used: Root, leaf

Cautions: Contact with leaves and stems can cause skin irritation. Avoid during pregnancy.

Season: Blooms April to September; it's best to harvest nettle leaves in the early spring and summer, as the leaves become more fibrous and tough as the summer progresses. To prevent the leaves from causing irritation and discomfort, gloves should be worn during harvest. Dry in a dark area until leaves are crispy and can be easily crushed or powdered.

Habitat and range: Moist, open sites, riparian and wetlands, near bodies of water; plains to montane; Canada to New Mexico and throughout most of the United States

Description: Perennial herb to 3 meters tall with spreading rhizomes and square stems. Leaves are opposite, serrated, lance to heart-shaped, 5–15 centimeters long. Flow-

Urtica dioica stems and leaves are covered with the "stinging" trichomes.
Janét Bare © Denver Botanic Gardens

ers are small, greenish, with 4 sepals and no petals. Male and female flowers may be present on the same plant. Seeds are lens-shaped, 1–2 millimeters long.

Constituents: Protein, linoleic acid, calcium, chlorophyl, beta carotene, caffeic acid

Medicinal actions: Diuretic, nutritive, alterative, anti-inflammatory, rubefacient, tonic, vulnerary

Cultivation: Stinging nettle grows well in sun or part shade. Prefers well-drained soil, that is rich in nutrients, especially nitrogen. Grow nettle in an area where it can be managed. Cut back midsummer to promote dense growth. Zones 3–10

Human use of *Urtica dioica* and other similar species dates to the Bronze Age (1,600 BC). Long considered a nutritious food source, a medicinal plant to many cultures, and a valuable textile, nettle is a useful plant of high ethnobotanical importance. The stems have been processed into netting, rope, and clothing for thousands of years, and both the leaves and roots provide a greenish-yellow dye. Though it grows rather inconspicuously amongst the lush summer foliage, a minor brush up against this plant can prove quite memorable. Stinging nettle contains hollow stinging hairs (trichomes) on the leaves and stems which inject histamine and other chemicals into the body, causing an itchy, painful reaction on the surface of the skin.

An infusion of nettle acts as an astringent and diuretic when ingested, while also fortifying the body with high amounts of minerals, vitamins, and protein. In fact, 1 quart of nettle infusion can provide the body with the daily recommended amounts of calcium and vitamin A and 10 percent of the needed protein. Nettle leaf can be dried and placed into a food processor to create a powder which can then be added to smoothies, soups, and baked goods for added nutrition. This nutritious herb helps strengthen hair, teeth, and bones, reduces cholesterol, and improves eyesight and digestion. A trustworthy herb for water retention, stinging nettle encourages the release of fluid from the body by stimulating the kidneys. Frequent and prolonged drinking of this infusion can dry out the body and may even cause kidney irritation. Herbalists recommend drinking nettle infusion sparingly, up to 1 quart in a 24-hour period, once or twice per week.

The practice of urtication, deliberately applying the leaves and stems of stinging nettle to the skin to provoke inflammation, shows promise for those suffering from rheumatism. Nettle leaves are a rubefacient, a substance that dilates capillaries, increases blood flow, and causes redness at the surface of the skin. Once an obscure folk remedy for treating arthritis or chronic and acute pain, urtication is becoming more popular as a modern alternative therapy—especially as clinical trials and medical studies are reinforcing the benefits of this ancient practice.

Nettle root shows great promise for treating benign prostatic hyperplasia (an enlarged prostate). Taken as a tincture or in capsule form with the powdered root inside, nettle root reduces swelling of the prostate and reduces obstruction of urinary flow. Nettle root, along with saw palmetto, is widely used in Europe for this purpose and is considered just as effective as prescription drugs.

Freshly harvested nettle leaves can be treated much like spinach or other leafy greens. Eating cooked nettle leaf provides more nutrition and energy than an infusion or tincture. Drying the leaves, boiling, or sautéing with fat on high heat immediately renders the irritating hairs on the leaf harmless. The leaves taste uniquely earthy and sweet, and make a great addition to soups, stews, and casseroles.

Nettle Pesto

The best nettle leaves for consumption are harvested in early spring and especially before the nettle begins to flower.

Ingredients:

3 garlic cloves, roughly chopped
2 heaping tablespoons toasted pine nuts

2 tablespoons grated cheese (any hard cheese will do)
½ to ⅔ cup blanched, chopped nettles
Salt
Olive oil
Juice of ½ lemon

Instructions:

Place garlic and pine nuts into a food processor and pulse until chopped and mixed. Add cheese and pulse until blended. Add chopped nettles, salt, and olive oil, and process until mixture becomes a paste. Finally, add lemon juice during the final mix. Pesto will store for a few days in the refrigerator.

VIOLACEAE/VIOLET FAMILY

Herbaceous perennial plants, trees, and shrubs with alternate or basal, simple leaves, irregular flowers with 5 sepals and 5 petals, fruit is a many-seeded fruit

Viola tricolor, Johnny Jump-Up
Jen Toews

VIOLET
Viola spp.

Also called: Hearts-ease, viola

Related species: *V. adunca, V. canadensis, V. nuttallii, V. orbiculata*

Parts used: Leaf and flower

Cautions: None known

Season: Blooms May to August. Harvest leaves in the spring and early summer. Harvest flowers at the peak of their bloom.

Habitat and range: Dry to moist, open or wooded sites, plains to alpine throughout the United States and Canada

Description: Annual or perennial herb. Leaves are typically basal or alternate and simple. Flowers show bilateral symmetry, 5 petals; 2 upper, backward bending petals, 3 lower petals. Throat of flower may show lines. Fruits are round capsules that can explosively burst open.

Constituents: Mucilage, saponins, malic acid, coumarins, vitamins A and C, essential oils, alkaloids

Medicinal actions: Demulcent, alterative, antitumor, astringent, bitter, analgesic, nutritive

Cultivation: Violets grow in full sun or part shade and prefer damp, well-draining soil. Sow seed in early spring or start indoors 8 weeks prior to transplanting. Violets typically bloom in the early spring, then go dormant during the hot summer months. Zones 2–11

Viola canadensis growing in a shady montane forest
Mike Kintgen

Nearly 600 species of violets grow throughout the temperate regions of North and South America, Europe, Asia, Africa, and Australia. For ages, this nutritive and healing plant has offered itself as a source of food and medicine to the people inhabiting these regions. The violet flower was hugely popular in ancient Athens, and it became a symbol of the city. Athenians infused violet in wines, used it for dyes, and prescribed it for a variety of ailments and diseases, even behavioral issues such as anger. Violet was used in England both cosmetically and medicinally and was commonly found in traditional culinary cuisine throughout France. Here in North America, many Native American nations use violet in a similar fashion. The Cherokee find the analgesic properties of violet to be useful for headaches and internal pain. The leaf is taken as a spring tonic. The Ojibwa reportedly use the plant for heart troubles.

Viola nuttallii growing in the plains-foothills transition
Mike Kintgen

Viola adunca growing in a sunny opening of a subalpine spruce-fir forest
Jen Toews

The leaves and flowers of violet are rich in vitamins A and C and are a great source of minerals and antioxidants. They can both be eaten raw or processed into foods such as jams, jellies, and syrup. The fresh leaves work well in a salad of greens and vegetables, or sauteed in fat with garlic and salt. They are traditionally eaten in the spring and may have a laxative effect on the digestive system. Eating too many leaves in one setting may cause mild intestinal upset, so it is best to mix with other greens or eat sparingly. Violet flower syrup has been considered a delicacy in many European cultures for centuries. The syrup is best when it is made with fresh flowers, collected in the spring or fall. Both the roots and seeds may cause nausea and vomiting; only the flowers and leaves are edible.

Violet flowers and leaves are a versatile medicinal plant, offering wide-ranging relief to minor ailments and can be processed in a variety of ways. The demulcent properties of violet offer relief for chapped skin, minor rashes, and stings, as well as inflamed tissues and dry lungs. A poultice, skin wash, or violet-infused oil are all worthy remedies for ailing skin. The mucilage in the leaves of violet works well on a sore throat and is considered an excellent expectorant for stubborn mucus in the lungs. A gargle of the tea can soothe coughs, hoarseness, and ease symptoms of the common cold and flu. Considered a cooling herb, an infusion of violet leaves and flowers can be sipped during feverish states, or to cool the body off on a hot summer's day. The small amount of salicylic acid present in the leaves may reduce minor pains such as headaches, styes around the eyelid, or pain within the oral cavity.

Violet Syrup

Violet syrup should be made from fresh violet flowers. The beautiful purple-blue hue is a great addition to beverages including sodas and cocktails. Before making this recipe, ensure the stems and calyxes are removed, leaving only violet flowers.

Ingredients:

1 cup water
1 cup violet flowers
1 cup sugar

Instructions:

Bring water to a boil. In the meantime, place violet leaves in a quart mason jar. Once water is boiling, pour over violet flowers, cover, and let them sit at room temperature for 24 hours. Strain out liquid into a saucepan, add sugar, and gently heat until sugar is dissolved. Place syrup into a jar, label, and store in the fridge for up to 6 months.

HARVESTING AND STORAGE OF HERBS

The practice of herbalism can be a simple, joyous activity which creates a meaningful relationship between the practitioner and the environment. Creating herbal remedies from plants that were cultivated and harvested from your garden or wildcrafted during a hike through the woods adds a layer of special importance to the remedies. A tea that was made from garden-grown bee balm is not only delicious but gratifying because the ingredients were cared for and nurtured. Using a liniment made from fresh arnica that was harvested on a hike carries much more significance than a store-bought product. Making remedies with medicinal plants teaches us that plants are much more than a commodity, but sentient, generous life forms that improve our health and enrich our experience here on Earth. With a few common tools and basic knowledge, harvesting plants for medicinal use is a very rewarding process.

Harvest from the medicinal garden
Blake Burger

When harvesting, use a pair of sharp, durable garden shears to cut the leaves, flowers, or fruit cleanly from the plant. To reduce the spread of disease, always sanitize equipment with soap and water or alcohol before cutting. Plants should be harvested on a dry and sunny day. Avoid harvesting plants early in the morning if dew or moisture has collected on the leaves and during or immediately after a rainfall. When to harvest is also dependent on what you are harvesting. As a rule of thumb, follow the lifecycle of the plant, harvesting plant parts at their peak. For example, if you are harvesting leaves, harvest in the spring or early summer when they are young and robust. Gather flowers at the height of their bloom before they begin to wither. Inner bark, such as willow bark, should be gathered in early spring as the plant begins to awaken, or in autumn as the plant begins to settle into dormancy. When harvesting roots harvest in the fall immediately after the first frost. Roots of biennial plants should be harvested in the fall of their first year of growth.

Observe the plant of interest before harvesting. Make sure the leaves or flowers are coming from a healthy, vibrant specimen free of discoloration, pests, or contamination. Harvesting the roots of a plant typically requires the plant to be partially dug up or completely removed from the soil. While it is important to harvest from a healthy plant, keep in mind that cutting the plant may compromise its health or even kill it. Thus, only take what is needed to ensure the plant can bounce back and thrive.

Drying Herbs

If your harvest yields an abundance of plant material that is in danger of spoiling, consider drying the plants to preserve their smell, flavor, and medicinal content. Drying herbs can be easy, requiring minimal equipment and involvement. The key to drying herbs is fresh, dry air with ample circulation. Avoid environments with high humidity to prevent mold. Excessive heat or direct sunlight can bleach color from the herbs and compromise the quality of the dried herb. Even after drying, plants should remain colorful, fragrant, and taste similar to how they would if they were fresh.

The easiest method for drying herbs is hanging them up to dry. This method is best for flowers and leaves. Tie sprigs or branches together into small bunches using twine, then hang upside down in a clean, dry environment with ample

Anaphalis bundle for smudging
Blake Burger

circulation, away from direct sunlight. To prevent mold growth, keep the bundles small, no more than 1 to 2 inches thick at the base. The amount of time the plant takes to dry is dependent on the type of herb and the environment in which the plant is drying. Check plants after 5 days, making sure the plant material is brittle and crispy.

Rack drying is an excellent alternative to hang-drying herbs, as fresh herbs can be dried more quickly, but this method requires more space, equipment, and labor. Any surface that allows for air to circulate above and below the plant is ideal, such as a mesh surface, wire racks, or muslin cloth. Space out individual sprigs, flowers, or leaves on the rack and place in an airy environment away from direct sunlight. To ensure even drying, frequently turn and flip plant material until it becomes very dry and crisp to the touch.

The method of oven drying herbs uses heat and air circulation to dry plants quickly. Plants such as thyme, rosemary, and sage, which are durable and low in moisture to begin with, are the best for oven drying. Also use this method when dealing with roots. To begin this drying process, turn the oven on the lowest temperature setting possible. Cover a cookie sheet or tray with muslin cloth or paper towels, and place leaves and flowers that have been stripped from their main stems and stalks on to the tray. When drying roots, cut them into ½-inch size pieces before drying. Place trays with plant material into the oven, keeping the door cracked to let moisture escape. After 30 minutes, remove the tray from the oven and flip all the plant material to ensure even drying. Place the trays back into the oven and dry for an additional 30 minutes, or until the plant material has dried out.

Storage and Preservation

To store dried herbs, keep them in compact airtight containers, preferably in dark or tinted jars with tight-fitting lids. When using clear glass jars, keep away from direct sunlight which can quicken the oxidation process of the plant material, altering the color and flavor of the herb. Dried herbs can last a few years when stored in a cool, dark place. Once herbs have lost their scent, or have turned brown, they should be composted or discarded.

TECHNIQUES OF MEDICINE MAKING

SUPPLIES AND TOOLS

Turning dried or fresh herb material into herbal medicine and remedies requires a short list of equipment and tools that can be purchased at most grocery stores or online. Herbal medicine making should be simple and approachable, but at times the process needs specific tools to ensure precise measurement and a quality finished product. Much of what is listed below is likely already available in the average home kitchen. However, consider purchasing separate equipment for your medicine making hobby. All equipment should be sanitized prior to use.

Measuring cups
Measuring spoons
Electronic scale
Cheesecloth
Fine mesh strainer
Mortar and pestle
Funnels
Mixing bowls
Saucepans
Double broiler
Mason jars
Amber dropper bottles
Labels

Infusion of nettle leaves
Blake Burger

SOLVENTS

Water: Water is an inorganic, tasteless, and colorless substance that makes an excellent vehicle for extracting the beneficial compounds suspended in plant material. From delicate chamomile flowers to seemingly indestructible reishi mushroom, water helps break down the cell walls of plants to release medicinal compounds. Water absorbs well into the skin, hydrates the body, and its cleansing action helps clear both organic and inorganic substances from surfaces of the body. As a menstruum, water is cheap, reliable, and readily available. Through diffusion and osmosis, water extracts minerals, tannins, bitter principles, starches, and carbohydrates from plants. Examples of water extracts include hot and cold herbal infusions, which are commonly referred to as tea, and decoctions. Hot infusions typically extract plant constituents faster, but the elevated temperature may degrade delicate compounds or accentuate bitter and tannic compounds. Cold infusions extract plant constituents using water at room temperature, a practice especially useful for drawing out mucilage and starches from plants. Keep in mind water does not extract essential oils and plant resins very well. Water preparations generally have a short shelf life, requiring refrigeration or a preservative such as alcohol to slow the growth of bacteria. Use high-quality spring water or filtered water free of heavy metals or impurities for the best tasting, healthiest infusions and decoctions.

Oil: Herb-infused oils are great for infusing plant material for cooking or cosmetic purposes. Because fat attracts fat, and repels aqueous compounds, oil is an ideal solvent for extracting essential oils, resinous material, aromatics, and flavonoids. There are a variety of plant-based oils available for medicine making including olive oil, jojoba oil, and argan oil. Each oil on the market has its own unique composition, taste, smell, and feel on the skin. Infusing plant barks, roots, and leaves in oil usually takes about 3 to 4 weeks at room temperature. The infusion process can be sped up by placing the oil-infused herb

Melt beeswax into infused oil to create a salve.
Blake Burger

in a warm-water bath; however, be careful not to overheat. Use dried herb or wilted fresh herb when infusing in oil to prevent mold growth. Herb-infused oils such as garlic oil, chili oil, or basil oil are excellent in the kitchen for sautéing, salad dressings, and marinades. For cosmetic use, calendula, plantain, and rose are just a few of the many herbs that infuse well in oil. These herb infusions can then be transformed into healing salves, lotions, and creams for the skin. Shelf-life of infused oils can range depending on preparation practices and the type of oil and plants used. To extend the shelf-life of an infused oil, store in a sanitized jar and keep in a cool, dark place.

Alcohol: Soaking seeds, roots, leaves, or other plant material in alcohol creates a highly concentrated extract called a tincture. Tinctures are meant for ingestion, but they can also be diluted for anti-septic purposes, or to fortify other medicinal preparations. Tinctures are safe to consume, easy to prepare, and convenient for consumption. The plant constituents that extract well in alcohol include essential oils, alkaloids, glycosides, and resins. For at-home tincturing of fresh and dried plants, 100 proof vodka is arguably the best menstruum for extraction. Vodka is relatively odorless and colorless, and at 100 proof, vodka contains enough alcohol content to extract alcohol-soluble plant constituents and also enough water to extract water-soluble plant constituents. Other spirits, including rum, whiskey, and gin, or beverages varying in alcoholic content from wine to 195 proof grain alcohol, work well to extract medicinal compounds from plant material. As a rule of thumb, sol-

Fresh hawthorn tincture
Blake Burger

vents with lower amounts of alcohol like wine or 80 proof spirits work well with dried or fresh herbs with low water content. Extracting using higher-proof spirits works well with herbs containing high amounts of moisture (roots, berries) and draws out volatile aromatics, resins, and oils. When stored properly in a cool and dark place, tinctures can last indefinitely.

Vinegar: Vinegar contains a high concentration of water and is highly acidic, making it an ideal solvent for extracting plant properties. Varieties of vinegar, including white, balsamic, and apple cider vinegar, break down plant material, extracting minerals, sugars, bitter principles, and other plant constituents, while also preserving them. Vinegars can be infused with culinary herbs, fruits, and vegetables to be used in beverages, dressings, or marinades. Antiseptic herbs, such as lavender and rosemary, can be infused in white vinegar and used as a nontoxic cleaning solution for the kitchen and bathroom. Medicinal plants, such as yarrow, astragalus, or calendula, steeped in vinegar make great herbal remedies for topical application and ingestion. An oxymel, which is a mixture of honey and herb-infused vinegar, is the perfect balance of acid and sweet, ideal for making a tonic or shrub, or masking pungent herbs that can be difficult to ingest on their own. When properly prepared and bottled, infused vinegars typically have a shelf-life of about 3 months, depending on the macerate. To extend the shelf-life up to 6 months, refrigerate herbal vinegars.

Honey: Honey is a versatile menstruum that can be used to sweeten infusions, used as a base to create syrups, or added to herbal vinegar to make an oxymel. As a menstruum, honey can extract minerals, tannins, bitter compounds, and aromatic compounds from plant material. Examples include honey infused with sage leaves which helps relieve sore throat, or chamomile honey added to an evening tea to promote relaxation and a good night's rest. As a natural preserver, honey can capture the aromatics from leaves and flowers, securing their potency while protecting the scents from oxidation. When preserving plants with honey, use dried herbs or plants with low moisture to prevent fermentation or mold from forming. Herb-infused honey can last many years when stored in a tightly sealed jar and in a cool, dark place. It is common for honey to crystalize or change consistency when plant material is added, but this change will not usually spoil the honey or impact its use.

MEDICINE MAKING TERMS TO KNOW

decoction: a tea made from boiling plant material, usually the root, bark, leaves, or flowers

electuary: finely powdered herb mixed with honey and molded for oral administration

essential oil: aromatic, volatile oils extracted from leaves, stems, flowers, or other parts of the plant

flower essences: made by infusing flowers or other plant parts in spring water and then adding alcohol as a preservative. The essences are used internally or topically to balance emotional states.

fomentation: a form of poultice absorbed in a cloth and applied to the skin

glycerite: a fluid extract of an herb or other medicinal substance made using glycerin as the majority of the fluid extraction medium

infusion: a drink, remedy, or extract prepared by soaking the leaves of a plant or herb in liquid

liniment: extract of the plant added to either alcohol or vinegar and then applied topically to skin

lotion: a semi-liquid preparation containing herbs and applied topically to the skin

oxymel: a sweet and sour herbal preparation made by infusing herbs into honey and vinegar

percolation: a process of extracting the soluble components of a plant with the help of gravity

poultice: a soft, moist mass of plant material, usually wrapped in fine linen, applied topically to the skin

salve: a semisolid preparation containing herbs and applied topically to the skin. Usually a combination of herb-infused oil and beeswax.

suppository: an oil-based herbal infusion molded into a small mass, usually inserted in the rectum

syrup: an herbal infusion or decoction with added sugar

Hops tincture
Blake Burger

tincture: an extract of the plant made from soaking the herbs within a darkened environment with alcohol for 2 to 6 weeks

DEFINITION OF MEDICINAL ACTIONS

adaptogen: works through the endocrine system to modulate the physical, mental, and emotional effects of stress and increase resistance to physiological imbalances and disease by strengthening the immune system

alterative: strengthens and nourishes the body, often through the removal of metabolic wastes

analgesic: relieves pain

anesthetic: induces loss of sensation or consciousness due to the depression of nerve function

antibacterial: destroys or stops the growth of bacteria

antiemetic: stops vomiting

antifungal: destroys or inhibits the growth of fungus

anti-inflammatory: controls inflammation, a reaction to injury or infection

antimicrobial: destroys microbes

antioxidant: prevents or inhibits oxidation

antipruritic: prevents or relieves itching

antipyretic: reduces fever

antirheumatic: eases pain of rheumatism, inflammation of joints and muscles

antiseptic: produces asepsis, removes pus, blood, etc.

antispasmodic: calms nervous and muscular spasms or convulsions

antitussive: controls or prevents cough

antiviral: opposes the action of a virus

anxiolytic: reduces anxiety

astringent: constricts and binds by coagulation of proteins

bitter: stimulates appetite or digestive function

cardiotonic: increases strength and tone (normal tension or response to stimuli) of the heart

carminative: causes the release of stomach or intestinal gas

catarrhal: pertains to the inflammation of mucous membranes of the head and throat

cathartic: produces bowel movements

cholagogue: increases flow of bile from gallbladder

demulcent: soothes and protects inflamed and irritated mucous membranes both topically and internally

diaphoretic: increases perspiration

digestive: promotes or aids the digestion process

disinfectant: destroys pathogenic microbes, germs, and noxious properties of fermentation

diuretic: increases urine flow

emetic: produces vomiting and evacuation of stomach contents

emmenagogue: regulates and induces normal menstruation

emollient: softens and soothes the skin

expectorant: facilitates removal of mucus and other materials

febrifuge: reduces or relieves fever

galactagogue: promotes the flow of milk

hemostatic: controls or stops the flow of blood

hepatic: having to do with the liver

hypertensive: raises blood pressure

hypnotic: strong-acting nervous system relaxant (nervines) that supports healthy sleep

hypotensive: lowers blood pressure

laxative: loosens bowel contents

mucilaginous: polysaccharide-rich compounds that coat and soothe inflamed mucous membranes

narcotic: induces drowsiness, sleep, or stupor, and lessens pain

nervine: a nerve tonic

nutritive: an herb containing nutrients required to nourish and build the body

purgative: causes the evacuation of intestinal contents; laxative

refrigerant: relieves thirst with its cooling properties

relaxant: relaxes and relieves tension, especially muscular tension

rubefacient: reddens skin, dilates the blood vessels, and increases blood supply locally

sedative: exerts a soothing, tranquilizing effect on the body

sialagogue: increases the production and flow of saliva

stimulant: increases body or organ function temporarily

stomachic: aids the stomach and digestive action

sudorific: increases perspiration

tonic: stimulates energy and increases strength and tone

vermifuge: expels worms from the intestines

vulnerary: aids in healing wounds

Source: American Botanical Council

HERBS CATEGORIZED
BY MEDICINAL ACTIONS

Alterative
Burdock
Common Dandelion
Lamb's Quarters
Nettle
Oregon Grape
Plains Prickly-Pear Cactus
Red Clover
Viola
Western Dock
Wild Mint

Analgesic
Arnica
Balsam Poplar
Black Snakeroot
Goldenrod
Greenthread
Pasqueflower
Pearly Everlasting
Prickly Lettuce
Viola
Wild Mint
Willow

Antiarthritic
Big Sagebrush
Yucca

Antibacterial
Arnica
Big Sagebrush
Black Snakeroot
Common Hop
Common Mullein
Dwarf Bilberry

Osha in bloom
Cindy Newlander © Denver Botanic Gardens

Engelmann Spruce
Goldenrod
Nettleleaf Hyssop
Oregon Grape
Osha
Pasqueflower
Pearly Everlasting
Rocky Mountain Juniper
Selfheal
Uva-Ursi
Wild Onion

Antifungal
American Licorice
Arnica
Arrowleaf Balsamroot

Common Hop
Goldenrod
Nettleleaf Hyssop
Oregon Grape

Anti-Inflammatory
American Licorice
Arnica
Bee Balm
Currant
Common Dandelion
Common Plantain
Dotted Blazingstar
Gambel Oak
Goldenrod
Greenthread
Marsh Skullcap
Motherwort
Mullein
Nettle
Nettleleaf Hyssop
Osha
Pineapple Weed
Plains Prickly-Pear Cactus
Skunkbush Sumac
Uva-Ursi
Valerian
Wild Onion
Willow
Yarrow
Yucca

Antimicrobial
Alderleaf Mountain Mahogany
Arrowleaf Balsamroot
Bee Balm
Gambel Oak
Wild Onion
Yarrow

Antiseptic
Balsam Poplar
Bee Balm
Common Plantain
Engelmann Spruce
Sweet Cicely

Antispasmodic
American Licorice
Catnip
Cleavers
Common Hop
Common Mullein
Curlycup Gumweed
Motherwort
Nettleleaf Hyssop
Osha
Pasqueflower
Pineapple Weed
Prickly Lettuce
Red Clover
Rocky Mountain Juniper
Valerian
Wild Mint
Yarrow

Antiviral
American Licorice
Nettleleaf Hyssop
Osha

Astringent
Alderleaf Mountain Mahogany
Black Chokecherry
Black Snakeroot
Dwarf Bilberry
Gambel Oak
Grayleaf Red Raspberry
Pearly Everlasting

River Hawthorn
Selfheal
Skunkbush Sumac
Uva-Ursi
Viola
Wild Strawberry
Willow
Yarrow

Cardiotonic
Motherwort
River Hawthorn

Carminative
Bee Balm
Catnip
Gray's Angelica
Sweet Cicely

Demulcent
American Licorice
Burdock
Common Mullein
Common Plantain
Elder
Rose
Viola

Diaphoretic
Arrowleaf Balsamroot
Bee Balm
Burdock
Butterfly Weed
Catnip
Elder
Gray's Angelica
Motherwort
Wild Mint
Yarrow

Digestive
Big Sagebrush
Chicory
Common Dandelion
Dotted Blazingstar
Gray's Angelica
Monument Plant
Nettleleaf Hyssop
Oregon Grape
Pleated Gentian
River Hawthorn
Sweet Cicely
Wild Mint
Yarrow

Diuretic
Balsam Poplar
Burdock
Butterfly Weed
Chicory
Common Dandelion
Common Plantain
Currant
Cutleaf Coneflower
Dotted Blazingstar
Elder
Gray's Angelica
Greenthread
Lamb's Quarters
Nettle
Oregon Grape
Plains Prickly-Pear Cactus
River Hawthorn
Rocky Mountain Juniper
Rose
Selfheal
Skunkbush Sumac
Uva-Ursi
Wild Onion

Emmenagogue
Marsh Skullcap
Valerian
Yarrow

Emollient
American Licorice
Burdock
Common Mullein
Elder

Expectorant
American Licorice
Arrowleaf Balsamroot
Balsam Poplar
Bee Balm
Black Snakeroot

Asclepias tuberosa
Jen Toews

Butterfly Weed
Common Mullein
Curlycup Gumweed
Elder
Engelmann Spruce
Gray's Angelica
Nettleleaf Hyssop
Osha
Pearly Everlasting
Red Clover
Rocky Mountain Juniper
Sweet Cicely
Valerian

Febrifuge
Big Sagebrush
Black Snakeroot
Monument Plant
Pineapple Weed

Hemostatic
Gambel Oak
Yarrow
Hepatic
American Licorice
Common Dandelion
Common Plantain
Lamb's Quarters
Motherwort
Oregon Grape
Selfheal
Western Dock

Immunomodulating
Goldenrod
Pleated Gentian

Immunostimulant
Cutleaf Coneflower
Elder

Laxative
Alderleaf Mountain Mahogany
Elder
Grayleaf Red Raspberry
Monument Plant
Rose
Western Dock

Nervine
Black Snakeroot
Catnip
Marsh Skullcap

Nutritive
Burdock
Chicory
Currant
Dwarf Bilberry
Grayleaf Red Raspberry
Lamb's Quarters
Nettle
Plains Prickly-Pear Cactus
Red Clover
River Hawthorn
Rose
Viola
Wild Onion
Yucca

Refrigerant
Catnip
Elder

Grayleaf Red Raspberry
Wild Mint

Rubefacient
Arrowleaf Balsamroot
Curlycup Gumweed
Nettle

Sedative
Black Chokecherry
Black Snakeroot
Catnip
Common Hop
Curlycup Gumweed
Gray's Angelica
Motherwort
Pasqueflower
Pearly Everlasting
Pineapple Weed
Prickly Lettuce
Valerian

Uterotonic
Butterfly Weed

Vulnerary
Common Plantain
Nettle
Selfheal
Wild Onion
Yarrow

GLOSSARY OF PLANT TERMS

achene: a dry, 1-seeded, indehiscent fruit formed from a superior ovary of one carpel. Used to describe the fruit of the Asteraceae formed from an inferior ovary.

aculeate: covered in prickles

acuminate: tapering gradually to a protracted point alluvium: deposits of earth, sand, etc., left by water flowing over land that is not permanently submerged

alternate: borne singly and spaced around and along the axis, applied to leaves or other organs on an axis. Also used to describe the position of floral parts of different whorls on different radii.

androgynous: having male and female flowers in distinct parts of the same inflorescence

angiosperm: a division of seed plants with the ovules borne in an ovary

annual: completing the full cycle of germination to fruiting within a single year and then dying

anther: the part of the stamen in which the pollen is produced

axil: the angle between one part of a plant and another part

basal: arising from or positioned at the base

berry: a fleshy or pulpy indehiscent fruit with the seed(s) embedded in the fleshy tissue of the pericarp

biennial: completing the full cycle of germination to fruiting in more than one, but not more than 2 years, and then dying

bifoliolate: having 2 leaflets

bipinnate: 2-pinnate; twice pinnately divided

bract: a leaflike structure, usually different in form from the foliage leaves, associated with an inflorescence or flower

bulb: a modified underground axis that is short and crowned by a mass of usually fleshy, imbricate scales

calyx: the outermost floral whorl usually consisting of sepals or a calyx tube and calyx lobes

capsule: a dry fruit formed from 2 or more united carpels and dehiscing at maturity to release the seeds

carpel: an organ, generally believed to be leaf-derived, which bears 1 or more ovules, a stigma, and sometimes a style. Often much modified in a syncarpous ovary.

compound: consisting of 2 or more anatomically or morphologically equivalent units

corolla: the floral whorl inside the calyx, usually consisting of petals or a corolla tube and corolla lobes

corymb: an inflorescence, usually a raceme, in which the flowers, through unequal pedicels, are in one horizontal plane

cyme: an inflorescence in which each flower, in turn, is formed at the tip of a growing axis, and further flowers being formed on branches arising below

dendritic: branching from a main stem or axis; resembling the branching of a tree

disc: the usually disc-shaped receptacle of the head in Asteraceae. Also the fleshy nectariferous organ which is sometimes annular or lobed and developed usually between the stamens and ovary.

drupe: a 1-celled fruit with 1 or 2 seeds enclosed by a stony layer (endocarp) which is embedded in succulent tissue (mesocarp) surrounded by a thin outer skin (epicarp)

elongate: lengthened; stretched out

erect: upright; perpendicular

filament: the stalk of a stamen below the point of attachment to the anther

floret: one of the small individual flowers of the Asteraceae or the reduced flower of the grasses, including the lemma and palea

flower: the sexual reproductive structure of the angiosperms, typically consisting of gynoecium, androecium, and perianth or calyx and/or corolla and the axis bearing these parts

follicle: a dry fruit, derived from a single carpel and dehiscing along one suture

fruit: seed-bearing structure formed from the ripened ovary after flowering

glabrous: without hairs

gland: a group of one or more cells whose function is to secrete a chemical substance

habit: the growth form of a plant, comprising its size, shape, texture, and stem orientation

herb: a plant which is non-woody or woody at the base only

hybrid: the offspring of the sexual union of plants belonging to different taxa

inflorescence: the arrangement of flowers in relation to the axis and to each other

introduced: not indigenous; not native to the area in which it now occurs

involucre: a large bract or whorl of bracts surrounding a flower or an entire inflorescence

keel: a boat-shaped structure, with a prominent longitudinal ridge

lanceolate: lance-shaped, much longer than wide, the widest point below the middle

leaflet: one of the ultimate segments of a compound leaf

margin: (in leaves) the edge of the leaf blade

mucilage: a soft, moist, viscous secretion

nut: dry indehiscent 1-celled fruit with a hard pericarp

oblong: an object in a rectangular or elongated oval shape

opposite: describing leaves or other organs which are borne at the same level but on opposite sides of the stem

ovary: the basal portion of a carpel or group of fused carpels, enclosing the ovule(s)

panicle: a compound raceme; an indeterminate inflorescence in which the flowers are borne on branches of the main axis or on further branches of these

pappus: a tuft (or ring) of hairs, bristles, or scales borne above the ovary and outside the corolla in Asteraceae and possibly representing the calyx; often persisting as a tuft of hairs on a fruit

perennial: with a life span extending more than 2 growing seasons

petal: free segment of the corolla

petiole: the stalk of a leaf

pinnate: with the same arrangement as a feather

prostrate: lying flat on the ground

pubescent: covered with short, soft hairs

raceme: an indeterminate inflorescence with a simple, elongated axis and pedicellate flowers

radiate: arranged around a common center

ray: the marginal portion of the inflorescence of Asteraceae and Apiaceae when distinct from the disc

resinous: producing resin; often sticky

rhizome: a creeping stem, usually below ground, consisting of a series of nodes and internodes with adventitious roots

rosette: a tuft of leaves or other organs resembling the arrangement of petals in a rose, ranging in form from a hemispherical tuft to a flat whorl

sepal: free segment of the calyx

serrate: toothed so as to resemble a saw

shrub: a woody plant usually less than 5 meters high and many-branched without a distinct main stem except at ground level

stamen: one of the male organs of a flower, consisting typically of a stalk (filament) and a pollen-bearing portion (anther)

stem: the main axis or a branch of the main axial system of a plant, developed from the plumule of the embryo and typically bearing leaves

stipule: one of a pair of leaflike, scalelike, or bristlelike structures inserted at the base or on the petiole of a leaf or phyllode

stolon: the creeping stem of a rosetted or tufted plant, giving rise to another plant at its tip

style: the usually narrowed, elongated part of a carpel or group of fused carpels, between the ovary and stigma

succulent: fleshy, juicy, soft in texture, and usually thickened

tendril: a slender organ formed from a modified stem, leaf, or leaflet which, by coiling around objects, supports a climbing plant

terminal: at the apex or distal end

trifoliate: having 3 leaves

tuber: a stem, usually underground, enlarged as a storage organ and with minute scalelike leaves and buds or "eyes"

undulate: with an edge or edges wavy in a vertical plane

variegated: usually leaves containing a pattern or marking of a second color, usually green and white

variety: a classificatory rank below that of subspecies

vein: a strand of vascular tissue

whorl: a ring-like arrangement of similar parts arising from a common point or node

REFERENCES

Ackerfield, Jennifer. *Flora of Colorado.* Fort Worth: Botanical Research Institute of Texas, 2015.

American Botanical Council. "Terminology." Accessed August 8, 2021. https://herbal gram.org.

Apáti, P., K. Szentmihályi, S. T. Kristó, I. Papp, P. Vinkler, E. Szoke, and A. Kéry. "Herbal Remedies of Solidago—Correlation of Phytochemical Characteristics and Antioxidative Properties." *Journal of Pharmaceutical and Biomedical Analysis* Vol. 32 (2003), no. 4–5 (Aug 8): 1045–53. doi: 10.1016/s0731-7085(03)00207-3. PMID: 12899992.

Bocek, Barbara R. "Ethnobotany of Costanoan Indians, California, Based on Collections by John P. Harrington." *Economic Botany* Vol. 38 (1984), no. 2: 240–55.

Bukovský, M., S. Vaverková, and D. Kost'álová. "Immunomodulating Activity of Echinacea Gloriosa L., Echinacea Angustifolia DC. and Rudbeckia Speciosa Wenderoth Ethanol-Water Extracts." *Polish Journal of Pharmacology* Vol. 47 (1995), no. 2 (Mar–Apr):175–77. PMID: 8688891.

Elpel, Thomas J. *Botany in a Day: The Patterns Method of Plant Identification.* Sixth Edition. Pony, MT: Hops Press, LLC, 2013.

Florabase. "Glossary of Botanical Terms." Accessed August 8, 2021. https://florabase .dpaw.wa.gov.

Foster, S., and C. Hobbs. *A Field Guide to Western Medicinal Plants and Herbs.* New York: Houghton Mifflin Company, 2002.

Franco, L., C. Sánchez, R. Bravo, et al. "The Sedative Effect of Non-Alcoholic Beer in Healthy Female Nurses." *PLOS One* Vol. 7 (2012), no. 7 (July). doi:10.1371/journal .pone.0037290.

Grieve, M. (Maud). *A Modern Herbal; the Medicinal, Culinary, Cosmetic and Economic Properties, Cultivation and Folk-Lore of Herbs, Grasses, Fungi, Shrubs, & Trees with All Their Modern Scientific Uses.* New York: Harcourt, Brace & Company, 1931.

Hutchens, Alma R. *Indian Herbalogy of North America.* Boston: Shambala Publications Inc., 1991.

Kartesz, J. T. "A Synonymized Checklist and Atlas with Biological Attributes for the Vascular Flora of the United States, Canada, and Greenland." Second Edition. In: Kartesz, J. T., *Synthesis of the North American Flora, Version 2.0,* 2003.

Kershaw, Linda, Andy MacKinnon, and Jim Pojar. *Plants of the Rocky Mountains.* Second Edition. Vancouver, BC: Partners Publishing, 2017.

Moore, Michael. *Medicinal Plants of the Mountain West.* Santa Fe: Museum of New Mexico Press, 2003.

Native American Ethnobotany Database. BRIT. (n.d.). Accessed September 9, 2021. http://naeb.brit.org/.

Nautiyal, C.S., P.S. Chauhan, and Y. L. Nene. "Medicinal Smoke Reduces Airborne Bacteria." *Journal of Ethnopharmacology* Vol. 114 (2007), no. 3 (Dec 3): 446–51. https://doi: 10.1016/j.jep.2007.08.038.

Plants of the World Online. Accessed September 15, 2021. plantsoftheworld.org.

Skenderi, Gazmend. *Herbal Vade Mecum.* Rutherford, NJ: Herbacy Press, 2004.

USDA, NRCS. The PLANTS Database (http://plants.usda.gov, 09/27/2021). National Plant Data Team, Greensboro, NC, 2021.

Wesolowski, A., A. Nikiforuk, K. Michalska, W. Kisiel, and E. Chojnacka-Wojcik. "Analgesic and Sedative Activities of Lactucin and Some Lactucin-Like Guaiano-lides in Mice. *Journal of Ethnopharmacology* Vol. 107 (2006), no. 2 (19 September).

Wu, Xin, Jing Shi, Wan-Xia Fang, Xiao-Yo Guo, Ling-Yun Shang, and Yun-Peng Liu. "Allium Vegetables Are Associated with Reduced Risk of Colorectal Cancer: A Hospital-Based Matched Case-Control Study in China." *Asia Pacific Journal of Clinical Oncology* Vol. 15 (2019), no. 5 (October).

ABOUT THE AUTHOR

Blake Burger is an Illinois native and graduated from Colorado State University with a degree in food science and nutrition. He has worked as a horticulturist at Denver Botanic Gardens since 2008. During this time he has created several medicinal gardens and spearheaded the creation of the Gardens' first Herbalism School. Blake is also a certified yoga instructor and leads several classes a week throughout Denver. During his free time, he practices yoga, enjoys learning about medicinal plants, and loves to hike, cook, and travel.

Subalpine wildflowers in Maroon Bells–Snowmass Wilderness, Colorado
Michael Guidi